MW01156502

I Am Not The King

By Allen Taylor

Unless otherwise indicated, all scripture quotations are from the English Standard Version

Copyright © 2020 Allen Taylor

All rights reserved.

ISBN: 978-1-7350735-0-7

"Scripture quotations taken from the New American Standard Bible® (NASB), Copyright © 1960, 1962, 1963, 1968, 1971, 1972, 1973, 1975, 1977, 1995 by The Lockman Foundation Used by permission. www.Lockman.org"

"Scripture quotations taken from the ESV® Bible (The Holy Bible, English Standard Version®), Copyright © 2001, by Crossway, a publishing ministry of Good News Publishers. Used by permission. All Rights Reserved"

"Scripture quotations taken from the Holy Bible, Berem Study Bible, BSB. Copyright © 2016, 2018 by Bible Hub. Used by Permission. All Rights Reserved Worldwide"

DEDICATION

I dedicate this book to my earthly father, without whom this story could not have been told. I am his only son, and he is my only father. He has taught me more about life than either of us were aware of at the time of the lessons. While the learning has not always been pleasant, it has always worked to my benefit. As I grow older, I see more of him in myself all the time and my desire for him is to know the peace I have found in Jesus Christ.

ACKNOWLEDGMENTS

When it comes to publishing books, the list of people to thank is always longer than the memory. Nevertheless, I'd like to thank the following individuals for their contributions to this work.

Melissa Hurd, for motivating me to finish it.

Nicki Jacoby, for being a gracious and critical reader.

Mom and Dad, who never knew they were helping me write my story but without whom this story could not have been written. The angry young man I was is not their fault, but they are largely responsible for the man I have become.

Tammy and Tonya, for being much better sisters to me than I have been a brother to them. Much love from the bottom of my shallow heart.

My wife's children. They are still delightful, even when they sin.

My grandchildren, a status that grows in number by the year. I have watched Dylan grow up to become a mature and responsible young man. May he continue to grow daily and honor God with his life. Savannya has a fiery spirit but a gentle heart. May her soul sit in peace on the lap of the Lord. Nathen was the first person to prove to me that love can be both unconditional and at first sight. His creative, intellectual, and mischievous inclinations mirror my own. My wish for him is that he will never forget the Creator who made him as he is and that being different, or curious, is not a sin. Live life with vigor, confidence, and faith in the living and resurrected Christ! Evelyn, as I write this, is a three-year-old pistol. With the cutest smile, she can bring the world to its knees. And the one on the way, surprise us!

My church family, who support and encourage me in ways of which they are not aware.

Bill Kimmel, a great friend who is always ready and willing to serve. A kind heart, if there ever was one.

My small group, for listening to me preach, and for being the best encouragers.

All of the people whose paths I have crossed. Some of them made it into this book. Many others have not. Yet, every one of them have become a part of my story. Most of them will never know it. But there are a few shining lights who have made indelible marks on my soul and never knew it. Mike Bangs was a much better friend than I was, and the best man at my wedding. He has now gone to be with the Lord, but I think of him often. DeWayne Anderton made me face my fears, and probably didn't know it at the time. Aaron Susek made me want to be a better man by his strength of character and quiet confidence, one of the humblest pastors I've ever encountered.

Because the last shall be first, I cannot leave out my incredible wife Theresa, for loving me when I'm unlovable. For tolerating me when I'm intolerable. For teaching me about family and helping me embrace one. My life has taken many turns, some of which have been with you and some of which have been because of you. Your beauty and intelligence still mesmerize me. I'm looking forward to our next adventure together. May I become better at all the right things and toss off all of the unnecessaries in our next chapter together. Thank you for making me a better man.

And, of course, the Lord Jesus Christ, who IS the King. Now and forever.

INTRODUCTION

In the first chapter of Acts, the resurrected Jesus tells his disciples that they will be witnesses of Him in Jerusalem, Judea, Samaria, and "to the ends of the earth."

And they were.

A "witness" is composed of two distinct parts. In the first case, it is an individual who has experienced an event firsthand. That is, he or she has observed something happening and can attest to the facts of the event. This component certainly applies to the early disciples, who were witnesses of Jesus' earthly ministry.

The second component of witnessing is tied to the first. The individual who observes can also then testify or give an account of that which he has seen. In that sense, every Christian is a witness.

We serve a living, resurrected savior. For that reason, Christ's work on earth is not done. He has ascended, but He is still present. His presence today takes two forms: First, in the power of the Holy Spirit, which indwells every believer; secondly, in the church itself as it lives out its localized, visible, and communal nature (what the New Testament refers to as *ekklesia* in the Greek). Collectively, we are the very embodiment of Christ and a witness to His transforming power.

The Lord implanted in my head a vision to publish my own testimony, the story of my life as it relates to the Lord, my rejection of Him, and my ultimate acceptance of His free gift of salvation. My journey is a wayward one. It includes many twists and turns, as many ups and downs, and a faith that continues to grow daily despite my own ability to get in the way.

This book is more than a memoir. It doesn't tell everything about me, or my life. It is a testimony to the power of God to reach the darkest places.

But it's more than that.

At the end of each chapter, I saw fit to include a list of discussion questions. Like many believers gather each week to study the Bible, often with a list of discussion questions, I encourage readers to start discussion groups around spiritual issues. Use my life as an example. In the same way that we study the lives of the apostles, the Jewish patriarchs, and the men and women of faith whose stores are recorded in the Bible, we can also study the lives of contemporary saints. Doing so should encourage us to walk in faith and strengthen our resolve to remain strong for our Lord. That is my hope in offering this book as a spiritual study in the life of a modern-day Christian—me.

In addition to reading my story of faith, I invite you to subscribe to The Crux, a newsletter I write about faith and spiritual issues. You can find it at https://thecrux.substack.com/.

If you have a desire to write and publish your own testimony, contact Crux Publications at https://cruxpublications.com/publish-your-testimony/.

Crux Publications seeks to be a faithful witness. Therefore, all feedback is welcome. You can provide that feedback by emailing cruxpublications@gmail.com.

Thank you for supporting us.

Allen Taylor
Publisher
Crux Publications

PROLOGUE

College classrooms are sterile places. Students by the hundreds occupy row seats as if catching the premier of the latest Star Wars movie or eagerly sleeping through another chick flick just to listen to some tweed-suited lecturer drone on about formulas, statistics, and office party trivia. In philosophy, the trivia is really trivial. One sunny spring day, I sat in such a class at the University of Texas at Dallas (UTD). It was in the spring of 1992. I was in my third year of school, and life wasn't going so well.

While discussing how philosophical systems compete against each other, and sometimes collide, the professor veered into a riff on Robert Tilton.

"Come on," he said. "How many of you have sent Tilton money?"

Robert Tilton was a prominent televangelist of the 1990s. In fact, his program, called Success-N-Life, was headquartered in Dallas and was the fastest growing television ministry in the U.S. in 1991. One of the chief proponents of prosperity gospel, he'd often interrupt his own legal tender-centered sermons and calls for financial gifts (people who mailed a check were sent a prayer handkerchief in return) to speak in tongues. I was not a Tilton fan.

But there was something unmoving about the professor's ridicule of Tilton and other televangelists. It spilled over to Christianity in general.

The specifics of the professor's lecture are lost on me today. The class was an introduction to philosophy. On this particular day, he discussed the contemporary philosophies of the early 1990s, mostly political. He compared Christianity to Feminism on the issue of pornography, pointing out that both were against it but for different reasons.

"Christians oppose it on the basis of an outdated morality while feminists oppose it because it objectifies the female body," he opined. Then he harangued Tilton.

I was confused. Wasn't this a philosophy class? What did bad religion have to do with it? Shouldn't he have been promoting the excellencies of Kant, Hegel, and men with unpronounceable names?

All around me, theater-style seats were populated by yuppies in training. Male and female, their religious proclivities hid beneath the veneer of their casual-but-conservative vestments. I didn't know these people personally, nor did I want to. At that time in my life, getting to know others was not a priority of mine. I preferred the solace of loneliness.

No one spoke up.

The law of averages says at least half of the students were Christian. We were in the Bible belt, after all. If anything, a good number of them attended some type of church most Sundays.

No one said a word. Except one skinny blond with long legs sporting short shorts. She sat on the opposite side of the classroom from me.

"How can people believe that?" she shouted. "How can anyone believe all that nonsense about God?"

Silence.

The professor let the question sit. After a dull measure of quietude, he continued. "Anyone want to answer that?"

A billow rose inside of me. I felt a strange urge to respond. I wanted to yell out to the far reaches of the auditorium ceiling, "Because they're intelligent!" I quenched it.

If you'd have asked, I'd have claimed to be agnostic. I might have given voice to atheism, if pressed hard enough. Or I might have just said, "Who cares?" It's hard to say because I tried not to think about such things.

Most of my hours were frittered away ignoring that still small voice deep within. In the caverns of my soul, there lay a seething volcano of hot ash, raw emotion, pure anger, and resentment, buried beneath the magma of my thought life. All it needed was one small tectonic shift to encourage it to the surface.

The professor pressed on. "Come on! I know some of you are Christians. Why do you believe?"

That was the first time since I'd left home, about eight years before, that anyone had challenged me to think about whether there might or might not be a god, let alone to consider the cross. Philosophy interested me because my parents' religion had not provided answers to my most pressing questions about life. I was searching for Truth, but I was running from God. And it was the unwitting scoffers of an atheist college professor who led me to the throne of Christ.

But I did not come to Christ that day. I did leave the classroom in the throes of a psychological funk, a sort of existential despair. I began, for the first time since entering adulthood, to ask, "Is there a God, and, if so, what kind of God is He?"

If there is a God, I wondered, *what did He want from me?*

Two weeks later, I went to the professor's office. I had a final paper due. Fifty percent of the class grade would be based on that paper. I was to pick a philosophy we had discussed that semester and defend it. I was struggling. Mentally, emotionally, financially, and spiritually. My entire being was filled with angst, rebellion, fear, doubt, and mysterious emotions I didn't recognize. I was in no state of mind to write a paper of the sort that college professor expected of me, and that felt strange because I'd never had a problem writing before that. I had never struggled with knowing what to think, how to think, when to think, what to think about, or communicate my thoughts in written form. I found myself in an intellectual stasis completely foreign to me. And I didn't know what to do about it.

I asked the professor if I could take an Incomplete grade in his class, which meant I'd complete the paper by a certain deadline and receive a grade then. The professor agreed, not knowing what was taking place inside of me.

As I stepped out of his office and into the sunshine, with the ceiling of Texas blue sky hanging over my head, my mind wandered to the next item on my agenda. I needed a job.

* * * * *

At the beginning of the semester, I had learned, my veteran's education benefits had run out. I'd earned those benefits while serving three years in the U.S. Army. The Veterans Education Assistance Program (VEAP) allowed me to contribute up to one hundred dollars a month toward college and the federal government would match my contributions two to one. There was a limit to how much I could contribute, but had I been better at managing money, I could have paid for four years of college.

My first semester of college was in the Fall 1987. If I had remained on full-time status, I'd have graduated in Spring 1991. But when a lucrative contract job that allowed me to work around my class schedule came to an end in 1990, a juggling act began. To survive and maintain my dream of completing a college education, I transitioned to full-time employment and part-time status as a student. Even that became more difficult as time went on.

I was working at a local service station one morning when the station's owner walked in and audited my cash register. I was a few dollars short, which meant that I had likely given a customer too much change. It wasn't significant, but noticeable. He grabbed my textbooks, sitting on the counter beside the cash register, and dropped them into the trash can behind the counter. My heart fell to the floor.

I looked at him, a broad-shouldered man with a pot roast belly old enough to be my father, scowling at me like an angry bird. My gaze shifted to his wife, gleaming starry-eyed like a lovestruck cheerleader. I bent down, grabbed my books, tucked them under my arm, and left the station.

It became evident to me then that this college thing wasn't working.

Writing was the only thing I knew how to do. Well. And it was the only thing I had any real interest in. But I needed a job, a means to support myself. I had no clue how to make money as a writer. In my mind, college was the ticket to my dreams, and I could feel it slipping away.

It didn't help that I had no support network. I had no advisors, no mentors, no coaches, no one guiding me or counseling me on things that mattered. And I had no interest in such things. In fact, I was trying desperately to avoid any hint of a meaningful relationship of any kind. I had made myself persona non grata to the very people who could have served in that role. I had done so intentionally.

There I was, no direction, no guiding principles, no moral or spiritual anchor, my one ambition nothing more than a specter of hope, tethered to reality like a runaway balloon. I was a spiritual and intellectual drifter, a complete unknown. Like Bob Dylan's rolling stone.

Eventually, a man reaps what he sows, and I certainly did.

One day, tired of couch surfing, I went to apply for an apartment. I was rejected because I had skipped out on one a year earlier.

"If you'll go back to the management company of that apartment complex," the woman in front of me said, "and make arrangements to pay back what you owe them, I'll approve your application to live in our complex."

I did that and worked out a payment plan for unpaid rent I owed. That company wrote out a letter stating our agreement so I could take it back to the place I was trying to get into. I learned an important lesson from that, but life did not immediately improve. There was still some gristle on the bone.

I went out to start my car one summer day and the radiator was dry. I poured water into it, but it ran straight through to the ground. Frustrated and alone, I wondered what to do next. I had just been hired by Time-Life Libraries to sell books and videos to people over the phone. I hadn't received my first paycheck yet.

Broke, brand-new job, no car, few friends, and no support group, I came to the end of myself. I ran into my apartment, slammed the door, and shouted to the nothingness I was sure was there, "Dear God, if you're real, show me a sign!"

Lost and confused, I didn't expect to see a sign. In fact, I didn't expect anything at all. I was simply blowing off steam. But I sent my request and figured the return on that deposit would be smaller than the interest on my bank account. I couldn't have been more wrong.

No sooner than the words flew from my lips, a mighty wind exploded over me. I saw no tongues of fire, but my tongue lit up like a fire. Tears streaming down my cheeks like an avalanche, I found myself standing in a dark second-story efficiency, my own personal upper room, stretching my arms toward heaven, clapping my hands, and praising God. In the frenetic uproar of my spirit, I fell back onto my bed and reached for the warm embrace of my Father. In the vapor of my mind, I could hear my own voice. What's going on? Why am I acting like this? Something mysterious, something unknown had come over me, almost against my will.

Matthew 7:7-8 says, "Ask, and it will be given to you; seek, and you will find; knock, and it will be opened to you. For everyone who asks receives, and the one who seeks finds, and to the one who knocks it will be opened." (English Standard Version)

I had knocked on God's door, and He opened it.

1 Corinthians 14:22 says, "Tongues are a sign not for believers but for unbelievers." (ESV)

Before that moment, I knew the story of Jesus, but I would not have called myself a believer. Days later, I pondered that experience, wondering what it could mean. I discovered that God had shown me the sign I had asked for. He sent His Holy Spirit to fill me, to reveal Himself to me, and he did it in a most gentle way. As instantly as it occurred, I felt an internal peace that I knew could only come from one source: God Himself. And I knew that something bigger than me had just laid claim to my life.

I was not the king of my life.

Discussion Questions

1) What do you think was going on inside the spirit of Allen Taylor, the college student, that caused him to squelch the idea of God?

2) Have you ever been frustrated by life's curve unexpected balls? How did you deal with it?

3) Do any of the other characters in this part of Allen's story serve as representatives of ways the world tries to mold Christians into the pattern of the world?

4) What happened to Allen when he began to praise God in his "upper room" experience? Do you believe the story? Is this possible?

PART 1

In the book of Revelation, a description of New Jerusalem indicates its streets are made of pure gold, so pure they are transparent. Like glass. It's a divine allusion to the prophetic city mentioned in the book of Ezekiel. The streets of Waco, Texas are a far cry from the streets of New Jerusalem, but I walked them.

My earliest recollections of childhood are in Waco. For the most part, they were happy days. It's where I cut my teeth on Dr. Seuss, where I learned to ride a bike without training wheels, and where I learned to end an argument with a hug.

I would learn other things in Waco, too.

Mom taught me the alphabet long before I entered school. In kindergarten, I breezed through the flashcards from A to Z while others struggled. On the first day of class, the teacher had us introduce ourselves by our first names followed by an animal whose name starts with the same letter. I introduced myself as "Allen Aardvark" and the class burst into uproarious laughter. I wasn't trying to be funny.

A year later, in first grade, Mom walked me to school on the first day. How proud I was strolling along with the most beautiful woman in the world at my side. Our neighborhood was safe, as I recall. Maybe even idyllic. A normal middle-class small-town suburb.

Mom pointed out landmarks along the way for me to remember my path by. She also encouraged me to look both ways before crossing streets, and to stop and wait when crosswalk signs indicated it wasn't safe to cross. The next day, and every day afterward, I was on my own. My first taste of independence.

The path was mostly linear. There was a red light a block or two from my house. The cross street was not a primary thoroughfare. If memory serves me well, it was a major artery for that neighborhood, but nothing more.

Four or five blocks up again, there was another red light. This time, a four-way stop. That was a major thoroughfare, and a left turn for me. The school was several blocks up. Though it began with nervous anticipation, it was an easy route to remember for a six-year-old and I became a streetwalking pro. I didn't need Ralph Waldo Emerson to teach me the value of self-reliance.

For as long as I can remember, I've preferred to work and play alone. In school, some teachers recognized that quality and would assign me special projects where I could enjoy solace away from others. In eighth grade, for instance, a science teacher put me in his private office and gave me a lawn mower engine to take apart. What I remember most about that experience was how systematic I was in removing every nut and bolt and placing them in a row in the order in which they were removed. The next day, I reversed the process and reassembled the engine. It was instructive as an exercise, but I haven't touched a lawn mower engine since.

It was experiences like these, and Mom taking personal stake in my early education, that turned me into a lifelong learner. It meant that I'd spend most of my life preferring books to people, and ideas to relationships. If there was something I didn't know but had an interest in, I could pick up a book and learn everything I wanted to know about it.

I've since learned there are things you can't learn from a book. Tying shoes might be one of those.

One day, while burying my nose in a book, my sister Tammy entered the living room and bragged, "I can tie my shoes." She pushed her foot along the floor to the center of my attention and grinned ear to ear. She was aiming to make me jealous.

It worked. At four years old, she could twist me up in knots.

At six, I could see Dick run without an interpreter. But I couldn't tie my shoes.

Tammy could. And she was proud of that fact.

My male pride wouldn't let her get away with having one up on me. I was the oldest, and in first grade, by golly. That clearly meant I must be the smarter of the two.

"I can too," I shot back. A lie.

We argued for a minute: "No you can't."

"Yes, I can."

"No, you can't."

Then Mom broke in. "Okay, why don't you show us."

What a wise young woman she was!

I figure now, the two of them must have been in cahoots. Mom knew I couldn't tie my shoes, but how effective it was to goad me into trying. And when I couldn't do it, she and Tammy laughed. Then Mom asked me if I'd like her to show me how. I agreed that she should do that, so she did. From that day forward, I believe I tied my shoes every day before heading off to school.

Playing in the yard with Dad was a regular delight. We threw baseballs and footballs to each other and had foot races along the sidewalk in front of our house. It seems like a normal childhood now, looking back.

Around that time, we had a neighbor named Mr. Tenpenny. He was retired. I don't remember much else about him, except that he gave me a pep talk one day after Dad exploded over something. Whatever set him off, he was fuming. I ran outside and saw Mr. Tenpenny sitting on his front porch. I sat down beside him, face longer than the driveway. He said something about Dad having a hard day at work and not to take it personally. I felt better after our little talk. Mr. Tenpenny was good at cheering up little boys.

First grade was also the year I had two girlfriends. Stacy and Kathy were their names. I'd walk them home from school and carry their books for them. Once safely escorted to their front doors, they'd kiss me on the cheek and bid me farewell. I guess that meant I was a decent gentleman.

Kathy was my favorite. She was the prettier one. When we moved over the summer and I ended up in a different school, she followed. I saw her one day in the lunch line. What a poetic moment it was to see her familiar face.

I don't recall all the details about the neighborhood we lived in, but it seemed like a typical American brownstone burb. Dad was a local truck driver of some sort. There was this long hill, a road, that Tammy and I would ride our bicycles down, and we thought that was fun. It was in that house where I learned not to run on wet pavement and not to ride a bicycle without shoes, both very important quality-of-life lessons.

The wet-pavement incident occurred when we were playing in the water sprinkler. At seven, I'd run and frolic without much thought about consequences. Once, I managed to get off the grass and onto the paved driveway. Wet feet, wet pavement, hard impact. That emergency room visit required stitches in the back of the head.

The "stitches in the foot" event is more memorable. I pedaled along with no shoes on my feet on a fine spring day. A chain link fence met the edge of the sidewalk where I was riding, and the bottom of the fence was raised a couple of inches off the ground. Somehow, my foot ended up under it. It ripped a big gash in my foot, and today I have the battle scar to prove it. I screamed bloody murder. The whole neighborhood heard it. One of the neighbors scooped me up, carried me down the sidewalk, and into the house. After that, I was on a first name basis with the emergency room.

There was another incident that occurred that year that would change my life, though I don't think anyone knew then just how dramatically it would shift the trajectory.

Tammy and I were invited to Vacation Bible School with some friends. We made birdhouses and other crafts, and heard about Jesus, but I don't think either of us drew the connection between Jesus and birdhouses.

On Friday, when we got off the church bus and ran toward the house, there was Mom, pretty and faithful, waiting for us.

"Did you have fun?" she asked.

"Yes!" we yelled.

Who wouldn't have fun building birdhouses out of lollipop sticks?

"Good," she said, "because you're going to church with your dad and me on Sunday."

That's strange, I thought. We'd never gone to church before. The following Sunday, we were in church, sitting next to Mom and Dad.

Life was very different after that. One day, Mom and Dad were smoking, drinking, and cussing. The next day, they were attending church weekly and doing none of those things. The transition may have been a little more gradual than that, but it seems like it was a sudden change. It was a positive change, but a change, nonetheless.

It would be many years before I'd learn the significance of that change. I think I liked it. The people at church were nice folks. The pastor had a son named Lester who was probably ten years ahead of me in age. I'd often sit next to Lester and follow along with him in his Bible. He would help me understand the preaching and allow me to hold his Bible, which was filled with highlighted text and pencil marks where he made notes.

One thing stands out in my mind about the Waco church. The kids would separate for Sunday School and the teacher would ask us to memorize verses. We were supposed to pick a verse, memorize it during the week, and share it with the congregation the next week. One Sunday morning, as we were getting ready for church services, I remembered that I was supposed to memorize a verse and began to fret. Dad suggested John 11:35, which simply reads "Jesus wept." He was proud of the fact that it was the shortest verse in the Bible, and he knew it. He wanted me to know it too.

I don't know why he suggested that verse other than that it was short. I didn't think anything about it at the time, but I have thought about it since. A part of me has wondered if he was teaching me to take the easy way out.

I don't remember if I shared that Bible verse on that Sunday or not—I think I did—but for many years after becoming an adult I'd look back on it and prod myself down a more difficult path for no reason other than as a personal challenge. It would be many more years before I'd realize Dad may have simply been responding to the short time frame that I was under and thought that verse a fit remedy.

For a brief time, we lived in a subdivision outside of Waco called the Texas State Technical Institute (TSTI). I don't know whether Dad was a student there or employed on campus, but we lived next door to our family friends, the Leidigs. Long before I can remember, Dad had befriended the man of the family, Richard. We called him Dick. Mom and Dad would play Pinochle a couple nights a week with the adult Leidigs while Tammy, baby sister Tonya, and I played with their daughters Rhonda and Melissa. Rhonda was a year older than me. Melissa was Tammy's age. They also had a son we called "Skip" who was much older than the rest of us.

One day, Rhonda and Melissa were at our house. We were playing house. Tammy and Rhonda were in Tammy's room. Melissa and I were in mine. I must have been in third or fourth grade at the time.

Melissa talked me into crawling under the bed. I had no idea what was about to befall me until she pulled her pants down to her knees. She coached me on what to do. Then the door opened. I heard Dad's voice.

"Allen?"

I poked my head up from under the bed. I could see disappointment in Dad's eyes. As Melissa pulled her pants up to her waist, Dad yanked me into the hallway and scolded me.

"Do you want me to spank your bottom?"

"No, sir."

"Then don't let me catch you doing that again."

Dad never said another word about the incident, but it left me curious, and somewhat apprehensive about my natural instincts. This emotional dichotomy, one with deep and stark spiritual dimensions, would come back to haunt me in later years.

I recall another brief incident that occurred while living at TSTI. Dad and Dick were sitting in our family living room. Mom and Dick's wife Carol had gone out. I was on my way out the door to play with friends when Dad called my name. With one foot out the door, I turned and looked. He held his hand in the air with a longneck bottle in its grasp and said, "Be sure to tell your mom." Dick sat in the opposite easy chair, looking like the Cheshire cat.

As I went on my merry way, I had no idea what Dad was trying to tell me. I could tell that he was upset about something.

Dick was a heavy drinker. Mom and Dad had been at one time. But after they caught religion, drinking became anathema. It could have been partly because Mom's biological father, Daddy Red, was an alcoholic, as were two of his sons. But the underlying narrative was religious dogma. There was a strict aversion to alcohol of any kind. Over the years, I'd learn of all sorts of rules that Christians were supposed to follow, and some of them didn't make sense to me.

Two or three years after this major change, we moved to Abilene so Dad could start a church. I don't know the details about how it came to be, or why, but, looking back, it seems like Dad didn't have the spiritual maturity to pastor a church. Nevertheless, we moved. We didn't see much of the Leidigs after that.

I was in the middle of fourth grade. It was not an easy transition for me. For starters, I didn't like my teacher. I also didn't have many friends, but there was one boy who became a classroom chum. We would draw mazes for each other on notebook paper and pass them back and forth during class. Some of the mazes were quite elaborate, characterized by narrow passages that took up one full side of a notebook page, and sometimes both sides of the page.

Outside of school, I spent most of my time playing alone.

I'd spend hours building race tracks out of common household objects. Rolled-up pairs of socks, rulers, Matchbox and Hot Wheels cases, glasses from the kitchen, Mom's silverware, books, various and sundry toys, mine and Dad's belts, and common household items. Whatever I could find. As I got better at building racetracks, I'd make them larger. Once, I snaked a track through my bedroom, into the living room, down the hall, through my parents' room, and around the outskirts of the kitchen. After building the track, I'd pull out my collection of Hot Wheels and Matchbox cars and race them around the house.

This would go on for hours. If the weather was nice, I'd play outside and make dirt tracks in the sand.

Another of my favorite self-entertainment activities was playing war with plastic cowboys and Indians. I had quite a collection. I'd pretend my bedroom was the setting of some old western. The Indians would take one side of the bedroom and the cowboys would take the other. I'd position them high upon shelves and furniture pieces, behind furniture on the floor, and create hiding places using the same household items I used to make racetracks. Then I'd roll up a piece of paper into a spitball and use it as a projectile. I was careful to ensure that each living cowboy and each living Indian got a shot during each round of fire. They'd pick a target, acquire its sight, and shoot. I'd toss the projectile from the position of the firing figurine toward its acquired target and if the paper bullet knocked a target off its feet, it was dead and out of the fight. I became quite systematic in my approach and kept it going to the last man standing.

My third way of entertaining myself was to play baseball or football with my sports cards collection. In those days, we could buy a sheet of awful-tasting gum that would come with five or ten sports cards. Again, I had quite a collection.

In my mind, these activities weren't just pointless fantasy. They taught me how to think systematically. Whether I was prone to playing alone because I had trouble making friends or because I was a pastor's kid, I cannot now say. It could have been both. But there were other environmental factors that contributed to my self-isolation.

For one thing, I was the oldest child of three and the only boy. By the time Tammy came along, I was accustomed to playing by myself. I don't know whether I had any friends at that age, but Tammy was two years my junior and I didn't have the slightest interest in entertaining her.

Another thing is, Dad had a temper. He could rage at the drop of a hat. As I grew older, the rages worsened. I have little recollection of them as a young boy, but memories of his hot temper while I was a teenager are still embedded in my memory.

And then there were the sermons. Every Sunday morning, and every Wednesday night. Hell. Fire. Damnation. I don't recall any grace.

The church consisted of our family of five and an older gentleman named Mr. Blackerby. Occasionally, we'd see visitors, but they didn't stick around past the first visit. Months went by with few visitors and none of them staying around.

That year, for Christmas, I received a board game called Monopoly. Except for Chutes and Ladders, I believe it was my first board game.

I loved Monopoly. We had fun playing it on New Year's Eve with Dick Clark's TV party playing in the background. It didn't take me long to master the game. I quickly got the idea that the goal was cutthroat competition through and through. It appealed to my bellicose nature. Kill the competition, winner take all.

Abilene was where I first learned to deal with bullies. There was one kid who followed me home from school almost every day. He rode a bicycle, and he had a big black dog that followed him around. The boy never did anything to me, but he looked menacing. One day, the dog got a little close to me. It wasn't vicious. It didn't try to bite me. But it frightened me. I think I was more afraid of the boy than the dog, but I was tired of that kid following me home every day. He couldn't have been up to any good. The dog got close to me and I walloped it on the head with my lunch box, a square tin cube with Superhero images all over it. After that, I didn't see that kid or the dog anymore.

The Taylor temperament burned hot inside of me. One day, I got angry at my fourth-grade teacher, an old lady who was probably a better teacher than I gave her credit for, and stormed out of her classroom, conveniently located near the front door of the school. I walked out of the classroom, out the school door, and all the way home. Mom was shocked when I walked into the house.

"What are you doing here?" She asked. I told her. And her response was prompt. "Well, you're going right back to school."

After we argued, she drove me to school and walked me right into the principal's office. He gave me a good paddling. He may have asked Mom's permission first. I don't remember that. If he did, I'm guessing she gave her consent because I do remember the paddle. And it was the last time I was spanked at school. At the time, I considered it an injustice, but I deserved it. I was a rash little boy. When I got home, I got another one from Dad.

I was not happy going back to the teacher's class, but I know Mom did the right thing. Returning me to school and forcing me to face the consequences of a bad choice taught me two very important lessons. First, quitting when you don't like the situation is not an option. Secondly, if you do something you're not supposed to do, then you must face the music. You may not like the beat, or the sound of the notes, but there are consequences to one's actions and, sooner or later, one way or another, you're going to deal with them. That was a hard lesson to learn, but an important one, and I've never forgotten it.

That was also the year I witnessed Mom cut her own hair. I don't think she'd ever had her hair cut before that, because I seem to recall it was long and beautiful. But something made her want to cut her own hair.

Being a part of the Holiness-Pentecostal movement, the church had strict rules about women cutting their hair and wearing pants, among other things. They may have loosened the rules and Mom decided to take advantage of her new liberty. Either that or she was in open rebellion.

I was in my bedroom when I heard her scream. I ran to see what the matter was. There she sat, in front of her bureau, with a lock of hair in one hand and a pair of scissors in the other. I'll never forget the look of horror on her face. Tears streaming down her cheeks, I've never seen her in that state of hysteria before or since. I don't know if it was because she cut her hair too short or if it was because she didn't cut it straight, or maybe it was the shock of seeing her hair that short. Whatever it was, she didn't like the outcome and it showed. I was scared for her.

While it frightened me to see my mother in that condition, the most frightening thing that year was a particular nightmare still embedded in my memory today. Since that night, I've only recalled a handful of dreams. I'm convinced it's because of this one nightmare.

It went like this: I stood in the street. All around me, balls of flames fell from the sky. Everything around me was on fire. People ran and screamed, trying to escape. Some of them fell to the ground as fire pummeled them from the sky. And there I stood, in the middle of the street, tears streaming down my cheeks, yelling, "Mom! Mom! Where are you? Mom!?"

That may not sound frightening, but to the eight-year-old me, it was sheer horror. I think it came to me because, for much of that year, I'd heard my own father preaching about hell fire and brimstone so often the images stuck in my head.

Before I knew it, Abilene was history, and we were living in Dallas with my Uncle Jay and Aunt Babb. Once again, my life changed dramatically.

There was much I didn't understand, but I would soon learn that I was very different from everyone around me. Family members I had known from a distance became permanent fixtures in my life. People I saw once or twice a year suddenly were present every day. Cousins, uncles and aunts, grandparents, and friends of the family. I soon became a member of a community, which meant the time I spent alone was severely diminished. Though it wouldn't be fair to say it disappeared altogether.

Almost immediately, I had playmates. And I'm not sure I knew how to handle that. I found that my mouth would attract the sort of trouble I couldn't avoid more frequently than my temperament would welcome.

It didn't help that I was the smallest male member of the family. All my cousins, even younger cousins, were taller and broader. And they loved to fight.

Uncle Jay, Mom's uncle, had adopted her and her four siblings when they were children. He pastored a small group of churches scattered throughout the state of Texas. He and Aunt Babb had three children of their own, one boy and two girls. Wayne, I believe, was the oldest. As far as I can recall, he only spoke three words to me throughout my childhood. One day, I tried to get his attention. I don't know why. But I kept calling his name, and he wouldn't answer.

"Wayne!"

I held a ball in my hand. Tossing it into the air and catching it, I called his name again. He didn't answer.

"Wayne!" Silence. "Wayne!" No answer. "Wayne!"

He was throwing a ball back and forth with one of my cousins. He turned his head and glared at me from under the brim of his cowboy hat. "That's *Uncle* Wayne."

I turned up my nose and walked away.

That's the only interaction with him I remember. He spent a lot of time teaching the other kids in the family to ride and care for horses. I wasn't interested in horses, so he didn't pay me much mind. I don't think I ever felt any loss from it.

His sister June was a regular at church while Wayne hardly ever entered the door. June taught elementary grade levels at one of the public schools in Dallas. She was also my Sunday School teacher during my teenage years. To this day, she's never married. But she knew how to make a little boy behave properly. Joy, the other sister, died in a car accident not long after we moved to Dallas, so I have little recollection of her. I'm pretty sure she didn't have children. Wayne's children, a boy and three daughters, were all older than me.

Uncle Jay's church became the center of our life. As a result, the cousins I spent the most time with were those who attended church with us. They were all younger than me. And if we weren't at church, we were at their houses.

One of our favorite activities, at least for us boys, was playing football. Players typically included my cousin Mark, a year younger than me; Mickey, two years younger; Mickey's younger brother Jody; Brian, a second cousin the same age as Mickey; and sometimes other boys in the church, or other churches within our denomination. We would split up teams and throw the ball around, usually playing the touch or "below the belt" variety because we were in our church clothes.

I was the least athletic among us, but I prided myself in having a very keen eye for detail and the ability to judge every situation with razor-thin clarity. Mickey had a temper with a slice of justice attached.

Quite often, we'd be on opposing teams. Of course, he was a good head taller than me for most of our childhoods. And we'd, almost invariably, have a disagreement over the outcome of a play.

"Out of bounds," I'd yell.

"No, I wasn't."

"Yes, you were," I'd shoot back. "I saw it clearly. Your little toe slipped over just past the edge of the side porch of the church about a quarter of an inch."

I could see it clearly from twenty feet away out of the corner of my eye with my head turned in the opposite direction. And Mickey was equally positive that he could judge from the centrally located position of being in the middle of the play.

The situations were always different. Out of bounds. Catch. Interception. Tackled, or "down," as we'd call it. But the outcome was always the same. My mouth would run, and Mickey would get to the point where he was tired of hearing it. It was then when he'd start throwing fists. And every time he did it took me by surprise. I just wasn't the fighting kind. For some reason, I always found myself unprepared.

I wasn't just unprepared. I was blindsided, taken by surprise, and bloody-nosed. And that ended the game.

Mickey would go away bragging, I'd go away crying, and the other boys would just go away. Thirty minutes later, we'd all be out in front of the church talking and joking, pretending like nothing happened.

This pattern repeated itself until we were old enough to control our tempers better. By that time, Mickey was interested in girls, and I was more interested in books. He went his way, and I went mine.

My first year in Dallas was also the year I discovered the love of my life. Two things stand out to me as pivotal developments that year. First, my Social Studies teacher—Mr. Ferguson—recommended me for the Talented and Gifted (TAG) Program, a Dallas ISD program for exceptional students. And the second was an English/Language Arts assignment. I was commissioned to write an autobiography.

I liked what we did in the TAG Program. Once a week, I was taken out of Mr. Ferguson's class and put into another room with twenty or so other students. We'd work on logic problems, conduct research projects, and perform creatively in teams on assignments such as video documentaries and other fun stuff that only eggheads would enjoy. The class was important to my intellectual development as it helped me hone my natural skills of critical thinking and creativity. But there was a drawback.

No one else in my world was developing along that path.

Mom and Dad were proud of me, but as I grew older and my critical thinking skills grew more pronounced, they became more of a problem. I couldn't understand why being smart was a bad thing, but it was. I'd hear things like, "He's got a lot of book learning but no common sense" and "he can read a book, but he can't turn a screw." As I grew older, such comments only served to spur me on. I wanted more of the book learning and less of the common sense. But deep inside, I craved validation.

By high school, I had developed a talent for the *double entendre*. I would speak over people's heads intentionally to show off my book learning, my well-read intellect, and the trivial knowledge I possessed about many things which have never proved much useful to me in knowing. And I had no shame about it. I spurned ignorance.

While I didn't much care for ignorance, it was stupidity that I had a real disdain for. To this day, that quality that causes a person to proudly display their ignorance as if it were true knowledge causes me to cringe. My father was the perfect example of it. The older I grew, the more I loathed it. If there was a subject that needed some conversation, or didn't, he had an opinion on it. And everyone knew what it was. The more he did it, the more I wanted to escape from it.

"The only person in America being discriminated against," I'd hear him say more than once, "is the white man."

He never tired of telling anyone who would listen, and far too many people listened, what he thought about any subject under the sun. It caused me to rebel with silence. I found myself holding thoughts to my breast that would have been better off expressed, just as an act of rebellion. I'd be anything other than like that, I resolved. You'd have thought someone had cut off my tongue. I preferred the pen.

Writing an autobiography was the first step to my development as a writer. That skill has given me a lot of opportunity over the years to get certain things off my chest. In college, poetry gave me a way to express feelings I had, and to discover feelings I didn't know I had. Fiction allowed my imagination to wander while nonfiction gave me clarity. And it all started at age ten with the encouragement of one or two teachers.

It sounds strange for a ten-year-old to have been taken so captive by things of the mind, but I enjoyed writing, and excelled at it. My autobiography was the seed that grew into my desire to be a novelist.

Fifth grade was a pivotal year in other ways too. It was the year Mom went to work for the first time. It was a net benefit, but there was one deficit: The Mom I had come home from school to for so many years was suddenly absent when I walked in the door. It had a major impact on me going forward, and I'm not sure that even I knew it then.

Dad had injured himself on the job and was out of work. He underwent a spinal surgery that led to a disk removal in the lower back and was hospitalized for a period. Eventually, he'd return to work, but the doctors told him he would never drive a truck again. They also said he'd never lift more than twenty pounds. To a man like my father, that news was devastating. His entire livelihood, and a major source of his pride, flew out the window on those wings.

The one thing I learned from both parents, and for which I'm grateful, is a strong work ethic. Both parents believed in an honest day's work, and they passed that on to me. Mom stepped up to support her family when Dad couldn't, but it wasn't easy. We lived on welfare for a short while before Mom could land her first job.

There was no way Mom was going to be content with periodic government handouts. She made sure to get a job and move us off welfare as soon as possible. And she didn't content herself with merely being employed either. She worked her way up to a supervisory position and retired years later.

Not coming home to a mother making dinner, however, did not mean that my sisters and I were left to fend for ourselves. We had a great-grandmother who watched us after school, along with several cousins—Mickey, Jody, and their little brother Jonathan—whose mother also worked. We called her "Mammy."

We thought Mammy was mean, but she was instrumental in helping us all to grow up. She was a strict disciplinarian. If any of us got out of line, or annoyed her too much, she'd say, "You want to go outside and get a switch?" And she meant it too. We would have to pick our own switches, and she wasn't shy about using whichever one we picked. We all learned the thinner the switch the more it hurt, but none of us wanted to spend a minute searching for one. And we all loved her home-made corn syrup, which she would mix up with peanut butter and serve on sandwiches.

So it was: From fifth grade on, my life consisted of three things: books, extended family, and church. And the three of them were intimately connected in me.

The centerpiece of it all was Dad. He grew angrier and more resentful. And the object of his ire was his own family. He always seemed to find something to rant about. If it wasn't politics, it was religion, or women, or blacks, or whatever happened at work that day.

One time, he pushed his way through the kitchen of our small suburban house—we lived in a small municipality called Balch Springs on the southeast side of Dallas—angry about something, and said to me, "I want this trash taken out by Thursday!" It was Sunday. On Monday, during another tirade, he walked by it and yelled, "I told you to take out the trash!"

A few weeks later, he was working on the family vehicle. On his back, under the hood, he yelled from the ground, "Bring me a crescent wrench."

Finally, I thought, an opportunity to play the hero. I ran to the chain link fence in front of our driveway, opened the gate, pushed my way through, pulled it shut behind me, and raced to the toolshed behind the house. I've got to get a crescent wrench, I said to myself over and over, lest I forget my mission. Upon reaching the shed, I jumped through the door and began filtering through the tools loosely organized in sporadic fashion, searching frantically for what might look like a crescent wrench. Then I realized, I had no clue what a crescent wrench was. I grabbed what I thought might be a crescent wrench and raced to take it back to my father.

When I got back to the driveway where he lay on his back waiting, I yelled, "Here, Dad." And I stuck the tool I had retrieved down toward the ground within his reach. He took it.

"That's not a crescent wrench!"

He pushed himself out from under the vehicle and lifted himself to his feet. Off he went toward the toolshed, the metal instrument I had just given him clenched firmly in his manly grasp. About halfway to the chain-link fence, he turned, face red as a freshly painted barn, and blurted, "Are you stupid?"

My heart fell out. Mom said nothing. Her fingers curled around my chin as she pulled me gently to her bosom. And for many years after, that word reverberated inside my head, in my father's voice. *Stupid.* It served as motivation, pushing me deeper into books until I drowned in them.

It took me many years to forgive my father for these outbursts. Even after coming to Christ, I struggled to forgive. I've learned that forgiveness is not a once-and-done event but is often a recurring act of mercy.

Dad had long since stopped attending church while the rest of the family continued our faithful and regular attendance. Sunday morning worship, Sunday night services,

Wednesday night prayer meetings, and Saturday night preaching. We seldom missed an opportunity to get away from his fly-off-the-handle escapades. It became our routine. It was such a normal routine by the time I'd turned thirteen that I'm not sure to this day that we were attending church for any real spiritual benefit or if it was to get away from Dad and his fits of anger.

Mom's and Dad's fighting intensified. I don't think my sisters, or I ever knew what their arguments were about, but they affected us on many levels.

One night, at the dinner table, they argued while Tammy, Tonya, and I ate. In silence, we each sat tending our plates. Suddenly, from out of nowhere, Dad shouted, "Fine! To hell with dinner!" And before anyone could react, the table flipped over and the whole family was covered in food. The floor carpeted with our evening meal, Tammy and Tonya in tears, Mom frightened and timidly holding her emotions at bay, Dad disappeared like a flash of lightning. I sat stunned, wishing I was anywhere but there.

Anger is a silent killer. Some families endure dysfunction in the bottle of an alcoholic or the needle of a drug addict. Others suffer under the hot fire of explosive temperaments. Rage is its own drug. My dope became books, ideas, and a search for an all-encompassing truth.

Meanwhile, we continued with the church charade. It was like we had two lives—home life and church. Dad was in one and absent from the other.

At one point, the adults decided to keep us children occupied with "children's church." We'd sing hymns, pray, and carry on like the adults in our own little version of church. In that setting, I'd preach sermons while the other kids sat placidly and listened. All the adults thought it was cute and were sure I'd grow up to be a preacher, following in the footsteps of my Uncle Jay. I believe I enjoyed it, but it was something I'd grow out of once the anger in me had built up enough to kill the desire. My understanding of theology was carved out by a small group of King James-only advocates with a raw sense of spiritual elitism. And when I had questions, they were often met with unsatisfactory answers.

I once asked Uncle Jay why the church insisted on using the King James Bible. He opened his leather sword and turned to the title page.

"This is why I believe he was a Godly man," he said, and pointed to the dedication to King James in plain black ink. I don't know what I thought about it then, but years later, I'd think it was absurd. After coming to the Lord, I began to compare different translations and note the differences between them. In most cases, they were minor.

Over the years, I've thought back to that environment that forged within me a grounding in biblical morality and a shallow belief in God. Today, I'm thankful I had that.

When I was fourteen, Mom and Dad had another one of their arguments. They yelled at each other, and ran through the house screaming, cursing, and shooting barbs like warring nations. During a ceasefire, Dad sat in a recliner situated in the corner of our living room. And sulked. I walked in and stared at him, curiously wondering what madness drove this man who was my father. I could not identify with him. He looked at me, almost in mockery, and asked the most dumbfounding question I believe I had heard until that time.

"I think I'm going to divorce your mother," he said. "What do you think about that?"

I didn't answer. But I remember thinking, *I wish you would.*

All I wanted as peace.

Years later, a friend of mine whose parents had never divorced, said to me in a group of young adults whose parents had separated, "Aren't we lucky?" I noted the irony.

A short time after Dad asked me about divorcing Mom, we started family counseling. I don't remember whether Dad enrolled in individual counseling, but I know Mom and Dad had some couples counseling, and I believe Tammy underwent some individual counseling. The entire family had several sessions of counseling, but I couldn't get into it. The counselor would ask me a question and I'd clam up. Even when Dad offered his platitudinous, "Be honest, son," I couldn't do it. I saw no reason for me to be there. I was not the problem.

As I grew older, like many teenagers, I began to develop my own ideas. I became difficult to handle. Arguments between Dad and me became more common. By the time I was sixteen, I was ready to leave home.

One evening, Dad and I sat at the dining room table in our East Texas trailer. We had moved out of Dallas the summer between my junior and senior years of high school. Mom and Tammy were behind me so I couldn't see them. I don't remember what the conversation was about, but we were having a family discussion. Mom said something and, to my ears, it sounded like Tammy talking. I belted out, before thinking, "Well, that's stupid." The words weren't far from my lips before Dad's backhand smacked my cheek. Startled, I ran to my room. "I thought it was Tammy!"

Dad knew how to shut down a problem. He was adept at causing them too.

On another occasion, I don't remember who started the argument, but Dad and I were having words. It got heated and I asserted my right to make my own decision. I didn't think I was being disrespectful. I was sixteen years old and hankering for more freedom. Dad invited me to take a step into the back yard. I took him up on his offer.

Dad was not a big man, but he worked with his hands. And he was bigger than me. He was a blue-collar man, and I was a scrawny punk. He lifted his arms to the ready. I knew I'd regret it the rest of my life if I punched my father. I turned, jumped into my vehicle, and drove off.

Not many days after that, he went off on another rant. After he stormed off, I sat next to Mom and confided in her a sentiment I've never expressed since.

"It's hard to love him and like him at the same time," I said.

"I know," she agreed.

I knew she wanted me to grow up to be a man, but not the kind of angry man my father was. The trouble was, I didn't know how, and there was no one to model it for me. I chose the easy path to not like my father. Over time, I'd learn I couldn't love him either.

Most boys grow up respecting their fathers, wanting to be like them. I've spent my life striving to be anything other than like mine. Even after meeting Jesus, I found it difficult to relate to my dad. He hadn't changed, and while I had the spiritual realization that a divine incarnation of the risen Christ had taken up residence inside of me, I found the march toward renewal of the mind rather slow. Over nearly three decades, God has turned my heart of stone into softened flesh. It was something I could never do on my own.

I've learned to be responsible for my feelings. Childhood events may influence my thoughts, but I've had to be accountable for my choices.

While childhood was full of disappointment and pain, there were also many joys. Playing with Tammy and Tonya, our cousins, and our childhood friends kept me grounded, though I wouldn't appreciate that for many years.

There are other memories too. One that stands out is of Uncle Jay taking me fishing. I don't know how old I was, but it seems I was younger than ten. I rode in the back of his pickup, which sported a topper, and he would talk to me on an intercom while driving. This was before the days of cell phones. It was a long trip and I have no idea where we went except that it was somewhere in the mountains.

I remember walking along a cliff and thinking, *Geez, I hope I don't fall off.* The best part about that trip was having the old man to myself.

There were also fond memories of Dad. He was a huge fan of Jerry Lewis. We'd watch Jerry Lewis movies together and laugh. We'd also watch professional wrestling. We'd cheer on the Von Erich family, who we considered the good guys because they were from Texas. As I grew older, I developed my own interests. They clearly were not the interests of anyone else in the family. I was different, either by design or by choice. Probably both.

My parents gave me a good grounding in biblical morality, despite the turmoil. They also taught me a strong work ethic. But most of all, they gave me plenty to think about even if I think now that I may have spent too much time thinking.

I left home an angry, bitter, sad, fearful, and broken young man. With no direction, I packed a bagful of ambition and a duffel bag with a ton of testosterone. Much of what I've learned I learned on my own, the hard way. I had no older brothers. None of the older boys or men in my life took an interest in me personally. Uncles were largely absent. I went from being a little boy to being a padlocked clam. Relationships were anathema to me, and I became my own worst enemy. Out of the shelter of mother's wing I stormed, raging like a drunk bird doped up on wild berries.

Discussion Questions

1) Does the picture the author draws of himself in childhood make you think that God could turn his life around?

2) How would you describe or define the spiritual environment of his childhood?

3) If you could sum up in one word the biggest spiritual challenge Allen faced as a teenager, what would it be?

4) Can you relate to any parts of his story?

PART 2

Toy soldiers have nothing on the real thing. They don't blindly follow orders, kill for God and country, or catch sexually transmitted diseases.

It was the summer between my junior and senior years of high school when I decided to join the Army. It made my dad proud. My best friend, an intelligent non-academic type named Jeff Allen, asked me why I didn't apply for a scholarship. When his father found out I was joining the Army, he exclaimed, "You're going in the Army?"

No one believed I'd be accepted, let alone that I'd want to join the military. I weighed in at one hundred twenty pounds buck naked and dripping wet. I had participated in no sports throughout high school, nor was I a participant in ROTC. There was no indication that military life and me would make a good match. Still, I saw it as my ticket to freedom.

While I graduated in the top ten percent of my class, I was an extreme underachiever. I did my homework in class and never studied at home after ninth grade. Had I applied myself, I might have risen to valedictorian or salutatorian. I didn't even know what those were.

For their own reasons, my parents didn't expose me to life. When my Aunt Joy died, they left my sisters and me with a sitter while they attended the service. Consequently, my first experience with death and grief was as an adult.

The first graduation I attended was my own. I didn't go to prom, Homecoming, or any school-related social events the entire time I was in high school. I left home socially inept and clueless. I was aware of this deficiency and let it inhibit me in many ways. It didn't help that Mom had sheltered my sisters and me, to the best of her ability, from any sort of influence outside of the church.

The legalism and family dysfunction shaped me and formed my outlook on life in ways I would not understand for decades. After visiting our church once, Jeff asked, "Do you believe you're the only people going to heaven?"

That was not the official doctrine, but I could see how he got that impression.

There were no mentors in my circle. None of my uncles made themselves available. Two were alcoholics. All of Dad's brothers lived in various parts of the country managing their lives and careers. Uncle Harold and Uncle Jay were dual-occupation preachers with families. Older cousins and friends of the family were all busy doing their own thing. Dad and Daddy Red nursed their white man wounds on unrealized dreams and country music. I was left to figure out life on my own.

Mom was emotionally available, but by the time I hit sixteen, I understood she could not teach me to be a man. There were some things I simply couldn't talk to my mom about. So, I didn't talk to anyone about them.

Because of my strict posture of self-reliance and reluctance to ask for help, there were no schoolteachers or counselors tuned in to my deepest needs. I entered adulthood a hollow shell of untapped potential, an overabundance of attitude, and with a broken rudder. I knew college was important, but my plan for college was three years of military as a vehicle for financing tuition. In the summer between my junior and senior years of high school, Dad took me to the recruiter's office, and I signed on the dotted line.

The U.S. Army had two programs that I took full advantage of. The Delayed Entry Program allowed me to sign up one summer as a member of inactive reserves and start active duty the following summer. After mustering out, I'd have two years of inactive reserve duty to complete.

The second program was VEAP. When I left the service in 1987, I had a fair amount of money saved up for college. Unfortunately, I had no plan for what to study.

Those three years in the Army were some of the most important years of my life in terms of personal growth and education. Three months of basic training put twenty pounds on my bones, entirely muscle.

As an afterthought, I asked the recruiter to put me in for airborne school. He didn't want to do it because it meant re-doing some of the paperwork.

"I can't guarantee you'll get it," he said, but he did the paperwork anyway.

For me, it was adventure. I was going to be an administrative clerk, figuring that would fit in with my natural skills. But I wanted to do more than push paper. As it turned out, not only did I go to airborne school, but my duty assignment was with the First Special Forces Group in Fort Lewis, Washington. It was the best duty assignment I could have hoped for.

My duty uniform included a green beret, an elite honor itself. I wore it proudly. I also got to rub shoulders daily with men trained for the most challenging work the Army had to offer. I learned to respect authority, and, more importantly, I learned how to command respect based on one's personal accomplishments rather than demand respect due to some feeling of deserving it. It was the best education money can't buy.

Dad surprised me one day when he dropped in on me during airborne training at Fort Benning, Georgia. I lay in my barracks room one weekend afternoon when the battalion day guard knocked on my door.

"Are you Allen Taylor?" he asked.

"Uh, yeah."

"Your dad is at the front desk."

"What?"

"Your dad is here to see you."

I didn't believe him. "You've got to be mistaken. My dad's in Texas."

I don't know why I found it difficult to believe him, but I did. It may have been partly because I wasn't accustomed to hearing from Dad. I'd been away from home at that point for a year and we talked on the phone once a month, maybe less. It was mostly because I had distanced myself from the family. I was trying to get on with my life, be somebody. But there was Dad, inserting himself as if he belonged.

The guard left and came back. This time, he brought my dad with him. As angry as I was at him, my heart jumped at the sight of him. I couldn't contain my expression.

"Hot damn!" I said and wrapped my arms around him.

I heard the guard gleefully say, "Alright!" It might have appeared to him that we were celebrating a happy family reunion. To me, it was a surprise, but an uncomfortable one. I didn't expect it, first, because it never occurred to me that Dad would just show up unannounced. He was a truck driver, so he would travel all over the country delivering tools for True Value Hardware. I should have expected it. I turned to the guard, thanked him, and shook his hand.

"Sorry I doubted you, sergeant."

Dad and I left the base for a couple of hours, which we were allowed to do if I was back in the barracks by curfew. We went to a local burger joint and made polite conversation. Despite trying to forget I had a father; it was nice to see him again. Years later, I'd wish I hadn't had such a big chip on my shoulder.

I was selfish. At the time, I didn't think so. I was simply living independently, minding my own business, exercising my American right to do my own thing. It may have been because I'd heard my dad preach so often that "you won't have us around forever; you'll need to take care of yourself."

He meant well, but it didn't sound to me like he was preparing me for life. It sounded like a scolding, as if he thought I was too stupid to make it on my own. I'd prove otherwise.

Three years in the Army were beneficial to me in ways I wouldn't understand until many years later. In addition to the rigorous preparatory training, I received upon enlistment and in airborne school, the daily physical training in a Special Forces unit was a cut above that of regular Army units. For starters, it was mostly done as individuals, so it required discipline. I had it. Secondly, all the requirements were above and beyond those of regular Army units.

Regular Army soldiers are required to pass a physical fitness test once a year. We took the test every quarter. Only one of those each year was a qualifying test, but we were required to meet the standard every three months.

We also marched twelve miles with eighty-pound ruck sacks on our backs every quarter. The standard was to complete it in under three hours, which I made a couple of times. In my first marches, I finished in three-and-a-half hours, eventually cutting it down to three-and-a-quarter, then to barely under three hours. Improvement, I learned, is a great motivator and a better confidence builder.

Another qualification was a 90-meter swim, which we had to do once a year. We did this in full combat gear, and I hated it.

On top of that, we had to jump from a perfectly good airplane once a month. In regular airborne units, soldiers jumped every three months. In our unit, the requirement was once a month. I loved it.

There was one jump when my parachute collapsed. It scared the living daylights out of me. It happened because I forgot which kind of plane I was jumping from.

The Army has two types of planes they use for airborne operations. C-130s are cargo planes and C-141s are passenger jets. We were taught to make a vigorous jump from the side door of a C-130. Otherwise, we would be slammed against the side of the plane upon exit, like Sylvester Stallone in the movie Rambo. With a C-141, we were supposed to just walk out of the door. If we jumped, we'd end up in the jet stream and it would suck the air out of our chutes. Up to this time, all my jumps had been from a C-130. On this day, we jumped from a C-141.

They told us everything we needed to know in our pre-operation briefings. We learned the weather conditions, type of plane we were jumping from, wind speed and direction, where the drop zone was, who the jump master in command of the operation was, everything important. I knew what kind of plane I was jumping from, but when I got to the door and was ready to exit, I forgot. I made a good, vigorous exit. The next thing I knew, I was falling like a rock.

Good training came to the rescue.

They taught us in airborne school to reach up, pull the risers away from our helmet, and kick our legs as if riding a bicycle. I did that, textbook perfect. My chute opened in time for me to prepare a parachute landing fall, which wasn't perfect but adequate enough to make my heartbeat again. God may have been trying to get my attention.

I had another close call. A couple of buddies wanted to get away one Saturday night. Stationed at Fort Lewis, Washington just outside of Tacoma, we drove up to Seattle. Sergeant Fredenburg, whom we called Fred; his wife; Private First-Class Dick Calvetti, pale-faced rosy-cheeked young man who'd become one of my best friends; and I hopped into my ugly Datsun hatchback, and off we went.

One thing everyone knows about Seattle is that it rains constantly. It doesn't matter what time of year it is; it's probably raining. It's also hilly. I drove.

We cruised around, looking for the residence of one of Fred's friends. He navigated. "Turn here, left here, make a right," and after a half-right turn onto a side street, and not knowing anything about the neighborhood we were in, my brakes quit working. We careened down a steep slope, picking up speed. It was drizzling rain.

I pumped my brakes. We went faster.

I pumped them again. The pedal eased to the floor. We sped down this quarter-mile slope, going faster and faster, and I pumped the brakes hard. I even notified my passengers. "My brakes aren't working!"

Everyone held on for dear life. No one said a word.

At the end of the run, we jumped across a T-intersection right between two trees. They weren't huge trees, but they'd have done some damage if we'd have hit them. We landed in a low spot on the opposite side of the cross street. As soon as we hit, the car's engine shut off.

"Anybody hurt?"

"I'm okay," said Calvetti.

"Me too," said Fred. His wife acknowledged her safety.

"Good," I exhaled. No one was hurt.

After catching our breaths, we tried opening our car doors. Fred had the passenger side while Calvetti and Fred's wife held up the back. The doors were barred from opening more than a couple of inches due to the trees on either side. We rolled our windows down and crawled out to get a look at the damage. Amazingly, after walking all around the vehicle, there was no damage. Not so much as a scratch. And all the tires were fully inflated. I couldn't believe my eyes.

After scratching my head and glancing at Fred and Calvetti, we all wondered what had just happened. I looked up at the crossroad above us and saw a police squad car drive past. We were just low enough in the ditch that if he glanced right and looked straight ahead, he'd have looked over my vehicle. He never saw us.

I sighed. Then I climbed back into the driver's seat and turned the key. The car started. I flipped on the headlights.

"Hey Fred," I yelled out the window. "Check my brake lights."

Calvetti moved to one side and Fred to the other. They both yelled the lights looked good. Blinkers worked, all the lights worked, the engine hummed smoothly. Everything seemed to work just fine.

I inched the car forward and tapped the brakes. The car jerked.

I did it again. No issues.

Now feeling like the Twilight Zone had arrived, I moved the car forward and onto the side road in front of me, which angled off from the crossroad over which I'd jumped a few minutes before.

"Hop in," I yelled, pulling the car to a stop. All my passengers climbed in, and we went back to the base. I drove slowly all the way home, tapping my brakes occasionally. No one spoke a word.

To this day, I have no idea what happened. The only explanation I can think of that makes sense is that my brakes got wet. Whatever happened, I call it a "God moment." I'm one hundred percent sure God was trying to get my attention, but I wasn't ready to turn my attention to God just yet. I was busy chasing American dreams.

Despite the harrowing experiences and the tough training, I had a lot of fun in the Army. And I met some great people.

One of the officers I worked for, Captain Varentes, had been a police officer before joining the Army. We sat around one day shooting the breeze with his boss Major Muench, who was the First Special Forces Group Surgeon. Captain Varentes said to me, "Taylor, has anyone ever sat around with you and talked like this?"

No one had.

"No, sir," I said.

I was due for an intra-battalion duty assignment in a couple of days, which meant that I would not be working with Captain Varentes and Major Muench anymore. Captain Varentes said, "Taylor, I'm going to miss you when you go."

I didn't miss a beat. I turned, and with a big grin, said, "Sir, you've got to learn to let go."

He and Major Muench bust their guts laughing at that.

I spent a lot of my time in the barracks alone, mostly reading books. But the soldiers in my barracks would get together on Friday nights in Sergeant Bennett's room and play poker. He had this octagonal poker table with a leather top and very nice wooden poker chips.

Most of us did it for the socializing rather than for the money. There were a few nights when I'd win, but most nights I ended up losing a few dollars. I set a limit to how much I was willing to lose and when I reached that limit I was gone. If I played my cards right, I could play for several hours before retiring to my barracks room.

Sergeant Bennett was the pro. He had grown up playing poker with his family. He'd count the cards, and the odds, and come out ahead on most nights. For the first time in my life, I felt like I belonged somewhere. Most of the men I hung out with were Special Forces qualified, elite of the elite. I was not. I was a support clerk, but they treated me like one of their own. There was no pretentiousness, no down talking, and no professional jealousies. We had a real camaraderie.

Some of the men were smokers, so Sergeant Bennett's room would be filled with clouds on Friday nights. One night, I pulled a pipe out of my pocket and lit it up. Everyone went bonkers.

"When did you start smoking a pipe?" Sergeant Weeks asked.

"Since you farts started destroying my lungs," I shot back. They all laughed.

"That smells pretty good," Sergeant Jernicke said. And everyone agreed.

From that moment on, the pipe became a regular part of our Friday night poker games. I even smoked it in my room on other nights when I was alone and reading a book or listening to music. I learned how to pack a pipe so that it would smoke evenly. And if I got the right tobacco, it had a sweet taste.

I didn't date much. Not that I wasn't interested. I didn't know how. I'd only had a couple dates in high school because Dad had grounded me so many times and for such long periods of time that I never bothered going anywhere. I learned to keep to myself, and that's what I did.

It wouldn't be untrue to say I was naïve. Mom's sheltering, the small circle of off-brand Pentecostalism, and Dad's bullying didn't provide very effective life success lessons. No one had taught me how to avoid a potentially bad situation, and I had no discernment.

I once took a couple of weeks leave and hopped a military flight from McChord Air Base. Such rides are free for active-duty military personnel, but the wait can be a few days. I made it to Oklahoma and bought a ticket from Lawton to Dallas where my parents would pick me up. As it turned out, my bus was scheduled to leave early the next morning, so I was stuck in Lawton overnight.

A local man entered the station and offered to sell me some pot. I hadn't had a joint since high school. I thought, *Why not?*

"Follow me," he said, and walked outside.

I thought we were going to his car. Instead, he led me down the street into a residential area. There were no streetlights, so it was dark. I started to get concerned. Dressed in my Class A military dress uniform, I stuck out like a green beret on a yellow elephant. The Class A uniform was a requirement for catching a military flight, and I hadn't planned on changing clothes until I got to Dallas. I really was wearing a green beret.

Just when I thought I'd ditch this guy, something flashed behind us. I turned to see a civilian vehicle with a flashing cherry on top. An older gentleman jumped out of the car and joined us on the sidewalk. He introduced himself as a reserve military police sergeant and showed me his identification. He explained that he drives the streets looking for military servicemen who might need his assistance. Fort Sill was nearby, so it sounded plausible.

"Where are you going?" he asked me.

"I'm on my way to see my parents in Dallas," I said.

"Who's this guy?"

"I don't know. We just met."

"Did he offer you drugs?"

How did he know that? I thought. "Uh, yeah."

"You shouldn't be out here by yourself," he said. "These local guys like to pick up young soldiers and promise them an easy high, then jump them and steal their money. I've seen it happen to a lot of unsuspecting young servicemen."

I looked at the long-haired civilian guy on the sidewalk waiting patiently for my return, and then back at the off-duty MP. I figured my chances were better with the MP.

"Why don't you come with me?" he said. "You don't want that."

I bid farewell to the long-haired guy and climbed into the passenger's side of the vehicle. The sergeant drove back to the bus station and parked. He backed into a parking space so we could see the bus station from where we sat.

"Want a beer?" he asked.

"Sure." What else did I have to do?

We sat in the bus station parking lot for about an hour, talking and drinking. Then the older sergeant invited me to his house for the night. My bus wouldn't leave for another twelve hours, but I wasn't sure I wanted to accept the offer.

"You know I'm not going to take no for an answer, right?" He chuckled.

He'd been a nice guy so far. "Okay," I said. "I should get some sleep."

He drove a few blocks up the road, parked at a curb, and we went inside a single-family residence. We walked through the front door, and he whispered, "My mother is sleeping." He led me to a bedroom at the end of a dimly lit hallway, passing a closed door on the way. "My mom is in that room." He pointed to the closed door. He opened another door in front of us. Once inside the bedroom, he closed the door. "She's got some health issues, so I look after her." After a short pause, he added, "This will be your room."

Naïve, no clue about how the world operates, and my guard let down after a couple of beers, I shrugged, undressed to my underwear, and crawled into bed. I thought the sergeant might leave and go to another room. He didn't. He undressed and crawled into bed next to me. It felt weird, and I don't know why I went with it. Lying in the dark, a stranger next to me, I wondered what I was doing. When I got to college, I empathized with feminist arguments that said when a woman says "no" mid-coitus and the man continues, it's technically rape.

Morning came and I felt used, ashamed. It was my fault. I had put myself in that position. I felt even more alone than before. For years, I tried pushing it out of my mind, but this new thing called AIDS plagued my mind.

I carried on, focused my eyes on college. With the family, I went through the motions. Show up, eat old-fashioned home cooking, and pretend to be a normal young man living a normal life. But deep inside, there was nothing normal about my life. And I knew it.

Back in the barracks with the men in Special Forces, all that mattered was the mutual respect we had for each other. I never told anyone about Lawton, Oklahoma.

Toward the end of my enlistment, I got into some minor trouble. I had been a good soldier. In under three years, I rose to the rank of buck sergeant. I had no marks against me, was in great physical shape, and did my job well. I had earned the respect of my peers, and my superiors.

Drinking was legal for me throughout most of my enlistment, but President Ronald Reagan had signed a law that changed the legal drinking age for service members effective January 1987. Six months before the end of my enlistment. Until then, the legal drinking age for service members was based on the state they were from. Overnight, I went from being legal at eighteen to being illegal at twenty.

In March that year, I went to an off-base party with some buddies from my unit. Of course, there was alcohol. When a friend of mine and I left the party, I gave him the keys to my car because he hadn't been drinking. I took a beer "for the road."

As we approached the base entrance gate, I tried to hide the beer between my seat and the door. The guard saw me and pulled us over. He arrested me on the spot for violating the base drinking policy, no open containers in vehicles. That led to my battalion sergeant major punishing me with a statutory Article 15.

Luckily, I didn't have any rank or pay taken from me, but it did mean I had one week of extra duty. A light sentence.

The unit had an appeals process. I could write an appeal letter and ask the higher unit's command sergeant major to overturn the decision. I decided to do it. It was a long shot, but I figured I'd try it. I had been encouraged to do so by a staff sergeant who had moved into the barracks after a divorce. "You've got nothing to lose," he said.

I really didn't.

I wrote up an appeal and sent it to the Group command sergeant major. At the time the appeal was sent, the Group command sergeant major was traveling, which I didn't know. In cases like that, the senior ranking battalion sergeant major performs the absent command sergeant major's role until the higher-ranking man returns. It just so happened that

Command Sergeant Major McGregor, *my* sergeant major—the man who had disciplined me—was acting command sergeant major of the Group. Just my luck.

Command Sergeant Major McGregor read my appeal and called me to his office.

"First, Sergeant Taylor," he said, "You're a good writer. You should do something with that." Then he went on to deny my appeal, giving me his reasons why. It hurt to lose the appeal, but I was glad to go through the experience. He was a kind, fair, and gracious man, and I respected him for his decision. It was something I could not do for my father, but I respected those who could handle their authority in an even-handed way.

I felt encouraged by Command Sergeant Major McGregor's handling of that situation. He recognized a talent I had and complimented me on it. And he knew I was not a troublemaker. I worked hard. And I wasn't a heavy drinker. I was just a young man, with a chevron of impetuousness on my collar, who had got caught in the wrong window of time. Those are the breaks. But the law was the law, and it was his duty to enforce it.

Not long after that incident, I mustered out and headed home. Reagan had signed an early-out bill that allowed me to leave the military six weeks early. I took advantage of it.

Once home, I enrolled in Richland Community College in North Dallas. I figured I'd save some of that college education money the military provided me if I took all my basic courses at the junior college level. And that's what I did. Then I transferred to the UT campus in Dallas.

I didn't have a plan, other than studying creative writing. I majored in Interdisciplinary Studies, UTD's liberal arts track. I took three poetry writing workshops and two fiction writing workshops along with studying philosophy and humanities. These classes had no practical career benefits, but I wanted to be a writer. As far as I was concerned, I could be a student for the rest of my life if I could figure out a way to make money with my writing.

I didn't.

Besides the coursework, I spent the rest of my time studying and reading various religious philosophies. I got into the Vedas, esoteric philosophers, and various mystics, and I combined that reading with excursions into astrophysics, cosmology, and whatever else I could fill my head with. I became mesmerized by the vastness of space. But none of what I studied had any practical benefit. I was searching for answers to life's deepest, most complexing questions, but I was looking in all the wrong places.

While enrolled at Richland College, I worked as a delivery driver for Mom's employer, Aetna. They used outside insurance policy writers and needed someone to pick up and deliver the work each day to their contractors. Since it was part-time, I could do that and manage my coursework. It lasted for a couple of years before the work ended.

There was a tall blond receptionist who worked at Aetna, and I thought she was beautiful. She was out of my league, but I could make her laugh. I asked her out one day and she agreed. I was taken aback.

"You want to go out with me?" I asked.

"Yeah," she smiled.

"Why?"

"I think you're funny," she said.

I didn't realize my sense of humor was an asset I could use to win the ladies. And I wasn't good at the follow-up either. So, I never closed the deal.

Meanwhile, I had run an ad in one of the weekly newspapers in town. I had started a discussion group. A man ten years my senior answered the ad and came to one of my meetings. He was one of the normal ones. Most of the other participants were a bit on the wacky side, even for me. One woman talked about this book she called The Urantia Book. It was allegedly "the truth about everything." I bought a copy of the book, with more than two thousand pages in hardback and small print and read enough of it to judge it as well-written nonsense.

Dewayne Anderton was good looking, intelligent, and outgoing. A paramedic by trade, he looked like the Marlboro man. He had all the qualities I desired but couldn't tap into. He was confident, good with the ladies, a smooth talker, and good at persuading others to do things they might not ordinarily take on to do on their own. I called him one day and asked, "Can you teach me to be a man?"

He paused. A few seconds later, he spit out his tongue and said, "Sorry, I wasn't expecting that. Sure, I'll teach you to be a man."

It was a strange friendship. He could pick up the girls, but he wasn't very nice to them. And he could string several along at once, keeping them all happy and eager to pay for his food, his beer, and whatever else they were willing to pay for. I observed everything he did, partly admiring his finesse and partially sickened by it.

On the one hand, he had a kind of power I didn't have. A personal power. He had a level of confidence that was natural and normal, but which didn't come so naturally to me. And I wanted it. It never dawned on me that such personal power could never come from anywhere other than inside me. I had a God-sized hole in my soul I was trying to fill, but I couldn't see that it could only be filled by the Being for whom it was designed. If there was ever a double-minded man, it was me.

If the one hand was the anvil, the other hand was the hammer. While I admired Dewayne for his confident demeanor, I didn't like how he treated his girlfriends. I wanted the power to pick up the ladies without the flare for manipulation that came with it.

In junior college, I had tried the girlfriend thing. It felt as awkward as lying with a man.

It didn't matter what I did, I felt awkward. Relationships were awkward. Social settings were awkward. Being around others was awkward. I eventually decided it wasn't for me. I had better things to do with my time.

While I tried my hand at it a few times, I had little interest in relationships. My temperament and self-centeredness got in the way. Plus, I pursued the wrong women for me. I had no clue how to go about finding a compatible mate, and when I found myself contemplating long-term connections, I'd look at the road map of my parents and realize that was not for me. Yet, my hormones were buzzing like a swarm of bees.

I turned to swinging.

It was hard to get in the door as a single man. Many couples, I found, weren't interested in single men. If I'd have been a woman, I could have a date every night. If I'd have had a wife or a girlfriend, doors would have opened. But a single man looking for hookups was difficult. Not impossible, but a challenge.

I found a niche in older women. Especially divorcées.

But I wasn't exclusive to the previously married. There were a couple of ladies with husbands who had caught my eye. I don't know what they saw in me. Maybe I was a distraction. Maybe there was something they weren't getting at home that I offered with no commitment and no strings. I never asked. For me, it was a way to practice my confidence-building skills at no cost to my ego.

It started in a topless bar. I hung out one night, killing time, drinking beer, wandering aimlessly through life. Of course, they keep the lighting low in those places. And its wall to wall lonely men gawking at women trying to earn a living with a product in high demand. Everyone hits on the dancing girls. Most of them get nowhere. But I was different. One of the waitresses, an older lady, caught my eye.

She approached me and asked if I wanted another beer. I put the longneck in my hand to my lips and swallowed the last drop. "Of course," I said, and placed my empty bottle on her serving tray. She scampered off to the bar to fill my order.

When she returned, I wrapped my arm around her waist, pulled her close, looked her square in the eye, and said, "You have a nice backside."

"Well, thank you," she said. I could tell she was flattered by the spark in her eye, but there was also a hint of surprise. At the time, I didn't recognize it, but I'd eventually come to know that spark as the look a married woman has when her husband isn't giving her the attention she craves. I'd also eventually learn how to exploit that look for my own gain. In Deanna's case, she was my learning lab.

I got her phone number. I called her. We hooked up once or twice. It didn't go far, but she later asked me, "What was it about me that caught your attention?"

I don't remember the answer I gave. It was some smooth talk I conjured up and she bought. But Deanna served me in the way I wanted her to. I learned how to pick up a woman. If there was nothing to lose on my end, older women provided me the boost in confidence I was looking for. A rejection meant nothing. They were old enough to be my mother, and married, so if I didn't get anywhere, big deal. Those times when I did, I felt better about myself. For a short while. I don't know why I didn't feel the same level of confidence with single women my own age, but I didn't.

The real benefit, in my mind, was that none of the ladies I was after were looking for long-term relationships. There was no danger of them pushing me toward marriage or ending up pregnant. I knew going in that each one had an expiration date, a shelf life. Some were shorter than others, but they all had one.

None of these stints ended on a sour note. When one of us got what we needed and the other was no longer necessary, we simply had a discussion, shook hands, and walked away. It became a way of life.

Still, my real passion was my dream. I wanted to be a literary icon. Again, I didn't know the first thing about getting there. I spent my hours writing. I thought college was the vehicle to my fantasy life. And that's all it was: A vehicle. Marriage, family, and everything else would just get in the way. My ambition was my family.

Married to my pen, I pushed it for hours, sometimes for twelve or fourteen in a day. If I wasn't sitting in a college classroom, I was at home stroking my ego with ink on white pages. And I was diligent. I took little interest in publishing, but I knew I had to spend my time honing the craft. And that's what I did. One slow pen stroke at a time.

In my first creative writing class at Richland College, I wrote a story and read it aloud to the class. Not only was the content shocking, but many of the class members remarked how in awe they were at the delivery. Some of them objected. Strongly. Others were amazed, in a good way. The professor was prolific in his praise.

After class, a beautiful blond-haired student of the opposite gender approached me and complimented me, telling me how well-written my story was. I wasn't used to that. I wasn't sure what to do. Tongue-tied, I let an opportunity pass me by.

At UTD, I took several creative writing classes. In the first one, a poetry workshop, the instructor assigned all the students dates for reading an original poem they had written. On my first assigned date, I read a poem I wrote modeled on another poem I'd read in one of the required reading texts. The instructor had us read a book titled *Satan Says* by Sharon Olds, a feminist poet who had been raised in a strict Calvinist home. Her book was the first book of contemporary poetry I'd ever read, and it opened my imagination. I wrote a poem that made use of visual imagery, and some provocative language, involving Satan, a poem, and me. It's what one would call an *ars poetica*, a type of poem about the process of writing poetry.

I delighted myself in making an impression with words. I was good at it. Better at it, even, than picking up older women. It became my reason for living, my purpose in life. A calling.

At least, that's how I pictured it.

In that poetry workshop, we were to pass out copies of our poems to each of the other students, and the instructor, the week prior to our assigned reading date. Each student and the instructor were to write their critiques on those copies and give them back to the writer on the day of his or her assigned reading. My poem, titled "Threesome," became a giant boulder dropped into a tiny stream.

One student, a practicing Buddhist, commented that the poem created its own music quite masterfully, but then he went on to criticize the content.

Half of the class refused to critique it at all. Some of them called the instructor during the week and asked if she could have me removed from the class. One or two others dropped out themselves. The instructor mentioned this when she introduced me, and added, "In literature, we are often confronted with ideas that we find objectionable. We all just have to play the game."

A typical liberal response.

One pretty blond my age who had decided not to critique the poem recited Psalm 23.

Another part of the class requirement was to memorize and recite a poem. The instructor gave us assigned dates for those recitations and this young lady's date happened to be on the same day as my assigned poetry assignment. It had to be another God moment because to this day I can still see her face and how shocked she was at having to be subjected to the cesspool of my imagination. She said nothing about my poem.

Another student, in classic liberal fashion, defended my right to write about whatever I wanted to write about. He gave no indication he understood what my poem was about, but he was willing to defend it.

I went home and read the comments about my poem. Many of them were insightful, some were encouraging, some weren't helpful, and a few were critical. I took solace and great pride in the instructor's comparison of me to Baudelaire, with an encouragement that I should read more of his poetry and draw inspiration from his style. Later in the semester, she confessed to me, after reading several of my poems, "I have no idea what you're doing, but it's working."

In truth, I simply wrote from the center of my soul. Two parts passion and one part imagination with a diligent attention to the right words in the right order. I spent every waking hour, and most sleeping minutes, learning to master the craft. I spent little time pursuing publication. Had I sent more poems, and short stories, to more reputable journals, I'm confident today that many of them would have found a home. I'd likely be a household name among the thousand or so working U.S. poets that are also household names in the same limited circle. I could feast on that accomplishment, as many poets do, until my dying breath.

College life, for me, was very different than for most other young people. Academically, I crafted a custom degree plan around independent study. It was a liberal arts degree by a different name, allowing me to focus on whatever I wanted to focus on, most of which had no practical benefit. When I got the urge, I found a fling. Then I went back to writing.

I had no one encouraging me. I had few friends. The ones I did have were a means to an end to me. Nothing more. And as I think back on it today, the primary driver of me then was fear. Fear of success. Fear of failure. Fear of exposing myself. Fear of losing. Fear of life.

And it hardened my heart to the things in life that give it substance.

One semester, I was hired to be a reporter for the campus newspaper. I decided to write a story on a psychiatrist at the school. He was testing a new group therapy technique. I decided to participate, thinking I might benefit in dealing with some of the anger seething inside of me. In my first meeting, an older gentleman discussing his pain confessed, "I killed my father."

That threw me for a loop. I looked at him, quizzically.

The psychiatrist explained that the man's father had died after they had harsh words and the patient was internalizing it. I realized my own struggles paled in comparison. The incident caused me to think more deeply about my relationship to my father, but I still wasn't ready to forgive.

My baby sister got married while I was in college. It was another surreal experience for me in a life of little reality. Everyone was busy with details. Everyone but me. I had no part to play. And I didn't really want one. In my mind, I was above all that.

As the wedding party prepared for the main event, Dad came to me and invited me to the back of the church to talk. I followed him along the corridors of the small church in the middle of a Dallas suburb to one of the classrooms in the back. Curiously, I wondered what idiocy might fall from his lips this time.

We entered the classroom and Mom busied herself with ironing a shirt for one of the wedding party members. Dad sat down. I sat in a chair facing him a few feet away.

"What I'm about to ask you," he said, his eyes bugged out, "is going to make you mad." He paused and looked at me, waiting for a reaction. I braced myself, sure that whatever it was he was about to ask was going to sound as stupid as he was already making it sound. "It's going to make you mad, but I'm going to ask you anyway." He repeated that a couple of times.

Okay, then, I thought. *Let's get on with it.* I tightened.

I wondered, though, as I often did when Dad talked, what's the point? Why would you ask a question you know is going to make someone mad, unless, of course, you intend to make them mad? I resolved myself not to let whatever it was get to me. I was not going to get mad.

Then he blurted it out, bold and proud as a hurricane. "Are you gay?"

It made me mad.

Hopping mad.

But I was not going to show him that. The last thing I wanted right then was to give him the satisfaction of knowing he had achieved his goal. My first thought was to respond, *Yes, Dad, I'm a flamer of the highest order.* I wanted to say, *When I leave here tonight, I'm hooking up with my black boyfriend and we're going to swing until the chandeliers break with envy.*

That would have pricked his brain like a pitchfork in a bed of hay. He had spent many hours playing guitar with Daddy Red, my mom's biological father, and discussing how the black man was taking over. Taking the white man's jobs, the white man's women, and the white man's whatever. Those two could write a book about how the black man was winning. I was certain that feeding that prejudice would kick my father where it hurt the most. But I didn't want Mom to hear it. I put on my best poker face and replied, "No, Dad, I'm not gay." And I walked out.

I went to the back of the church without saying a word to anyone and slumped on the back pew. No one said a word to me for the rest of the event. After the ceremony, I gathered with everyone at the door of the church and threw rice at the newlywed couple embarking upon their life journey together. Then I went home and cried.

There have only been a handful of times in my life, and I can count them on one hand, when I felt the sudden urge to plow my knuckles into somebody else's face. That moment in the back classroom of the church was one of them. It became another brick in the fortress I had built around my heart.

After that, I made myself scarcer at family events. Had Mom not chosen to remain married to Dad, I'd have stayed away from him completely. He became the most loathsome face in my world. His voice became the song that would never end. You know that song you absolutely hate but can't get out of your mind? You find yourself singing it even when there's no music. And when you catch yourself, you try feverishly to replace it with something else, *anything* else. That song was my dad's voice. I heard it everywhere I went.

There were days I'd hear it ask, *are you gay?* Other days, it would simply say, *you'll never amount to anything.* Or I'd hear, *what are you, stupid?* It was never positive. It was never good. It was pervasive.

The times I did go around the family were simply to see my sisters and my mom. But I didn't speak much. We certainly never talked about anything meaningful. I'd be cordial with my dad, but I didn't go out of my way to give him any special attention, nor did he me. Most of my time was spent trying to push him out of my mind, only to find that the more I tried the more his voice and his face penetrated my conscience. I was a walking cauldron of hot lava.

Not only did I not have any interest in relationships, but if I had had an interest, I wasn't emotionally equipped to handle one. I made every effort I could to be anything but like my father. And the more I tried, the more I failed.

There was a time when I needed work, so I got a job as a salesman. I was lousy at it. I had applied for a position as an encyclopedia salesman for Encyclopedia Britannica. In my mind, they were the best encyclopedias on the planet. I believed in them. If I was going to sell something, it had to be something I could believe in. But I was no salesman. I didn't sell a single set of encyclopedias.

One day, dressed up in suit and tie, I was all set to drive to an appointment with a prospect. At the time, I shared an apartment with Tammy. We also shared a vehicle together for a few weeks, though it was in her name. I put the key in the ignition, pulled out of my parking space, and the car stalled. It wouldn't start again. I lost my temper and gave the driver's side window a swift roundhouse. The window shattered all over the vehicle.

I called my mom, and she came to the rescue. When she saw the window, she asked, "What happened?" I told her. She laid into me hard. "You criticize your daddy for that kind of behavior, and you can't control yourself any better! That was stupid."

She was right. I felt bad. I've looked back on that moment often just to catch a glimpse of what I don't want to be. It's served as motivation to control my temper. At times, I've succeeded; other times, I have not. As I've grown older, the successes have come more often. I still look back at that moment at times when I feel a rush of emotion. I pray to God, and it quickly fades.

But I was powerless then against it. I couldn't control it. I didn't try.

Anger, sexual urges, pride, I had it all. I poured it all into poetry, stories, and my loins. Writing became my outlet. Sex became my recreation. I kept both a secret. What my family didn't know wouldn't hurt them. I knew Mom wouldn't approve, and Dad would just make sarcastic, caustic remarks. I didn't care what Tammy or Tonya thought. They were on their own. I was my own god.

I picked up pot smoking. It was better than alcohol. It eased my mind, mellowed me out. I didn't feel like hitting things, and I didn't feel like yelling at the world. At first, it was casual. Then daily.

To me, marijuana was something I could do at home in the evenings before going to bed. It was also nice to share with someone I was about to share my body with. And I could get high and write some beautiful lines of poetry. But I never took it in public with me or went out in public after smoking. That would have been crossing a line.

Sexually, I oscillated between feeding the urge and feeling guilty, or squelching it. When guilt would set in, I'd take a break. When I'd get the urge again, I'd give in or pour myself into my writing. Between bouts of hitting on older women, I found myself entertaining male attractions. When those feelings started creeping in, I'd remember Lawton, Oklahoma and either feed the older woman urge or grip the pen tighter. But it became more difficult to resist.

Once, I met a man who asked for a ride to a friend's house. He lived in the same neighborhood with me. I was going the direction he wanted to go, so I agreed.

During the drive, he made conversation. "You look familiar," he grinned.

I chuckled. *Yeah, right.*

"Have you ever been checked for a hernia?" he asked. He was a medical professional of some sort and said he thought he might have seen me in the office of the doctor for whom he worked. I replied that I had not.

He was a talker. I was cautious. And not very trusting.

Before we got to his destination, he talked me into pulling off into a wooded area behind an apartment complex. We walked off into the woods and returned to the vehicle a few minutes later. It wasn't much to speak of, but a few days later there was a sore on the tip of my penis.

I booked a doctor's appointment. The doctor said it could be a viral infection, or something to that effect. I knew what caused it. I did some research of my own and narrowed it down to either syphilis or herpes. Then I did something stupid.

Nothing.

It was a mix of shame and pride that kept me from going to another doctor or seeking advice elsewhere. If it was herpes, I thought, it would return. Then I'd know for sure. What I ignored was that syphilis is deadly. The sore goes away and doesn't return, but the disease continues to remain active in the body and eventually makes its way to the brain where it eats away at the gray matter. I watched to see if the sore would return.

And kept writing.

Pride goes before the fall, and I had an extra dose of it. Living the dream. By day, I was in school, cavorting with intellectuals. Between classes, and on weekends, I wrote poetry and fiction. Occasionally, I'd get proud of something I wrote and send it to a publisher. A few times, I managed a credit. Most times, I did not. College money from the Army's VEAP program ensured I didn't have to worry about money for rent and utilities. For a couple of years, I managed to earn some running around money by delivering insurance documents back and forth between Aetna and several insurance policy writers working from home. That took up a couple of hours a day. The rest of the time I was free.

That worked well until I transferred to UTD. The first year was great. Then the VEAP money ran out. But I was still in my head.

One Saturday, I visited my parents in East Texas. I always went alone. I was managing "the buckets" of my life. College was one. Writing was one. Family was one. Extracurricular activities had their own. There was no bucket for relationships.

While at my parents' house, I just lay around most of the time. Quite often, I'd lean back on the sofa and drift off to sleep. Of course, Mom would make us a meal. And we'd spend some time hanging out. Dad liked to play backgammon so we'd sometimes get into a game that might take up some time. But we never talked about anything meaningful.

This one time, I believe it was just Mom and Dad, and me. Tammy and Tonya had their families. I lounged on the sofa. When I raised up, after having dozed for a few minutes, Dad was sitting on a chair watching me.

"Can I ask you a question?" he asked. And before I could respond, he hit me with it. "Are you ashamed of us?"

I groaned, then I lay back on the sofa and shut my eyes. I never answered him.

It was rude of me. Here he was, trying to reach out to me, and I was avoiding it. I was too busy trying not to be involved emotionally. The fact is a part of me was ashamed. But mostly, I was angry. I tried hard not to show it, but inside was a grumbling volcano of hate and resentment. I hated my father and didn't have the guts to say it.

There was a part of the anger that was also directed at Mom. I hated that she chose to stay married to Dad. In my mind, she had every reason to seek a divorce if she wanted it. She didn't want it, and it pissed me off.

I tried a few times to talk to her about it. She would only say, "I don't believe in divorce. God doesn't like that."

She got that from Malachi 2:16. The text reads, "'For I hate divorce,' says the LORD, the God of Israel. 'He who divorces his wife covers his garment with violence,' says the LORD of Hosts."

Another verse she liked to quote was Mark 10:9. "Therefore what God has joined together, let not man put asunder." She loved quoting the King James translation. Every other Bible translation was anathema. Anything that wasn't King James was seen as a violation of Revelation 22: 18-19.

Mom's legalistic insistence that divorce was not right under any circumstances seemed irrational to me, and it made me despise her. I found myself at times thinking I'd visit her more often if she did pursue a divorce, but I never told her so. I didn't want to pressure her into doing what she didn't want to do. At the same time, I secretly hoped she'd ditch the man she was married to. And I grew increasingly distrusting and disrespectful toward the institution of marriage. It wasn't natural, I'd tell myself.

There I was, a total wreck of a man. On the outside, it appeared I had it together. On the inside, I was a mess.

On another occasion, while visiting the family in East Texas, I had gone out drinking. I don't remember if I was with myself or one of my sisters, but I'd had a few beers. And something happened that upset me. I don't remember what. The part I remember is leaving to go home with a harbor of pain in my impoverished soul. I wouldn't talk about it with anyone. I was on my way home to nurse my perceived wound with the drug better than drugs. My pen.

The visibility on the dark East Texas roads between my parents' place and the concrete slab of Dallas, which I called home, was very low. And it was raining. Those forces coupled with my lowered ability to think straight through the lens of my two-beer limit, and the tears I was unsuccessfully fighting to restrain, caused me to lose control of my vehicle. I found myself sliding across the two-lane country road, across a ditch, and through an electric fence into a pasture. My vehicle spun so that I was facing the road, but I was about fifty feet off the paved path in somebody's huge plot of empty acreage.

After regaining my composure, I looked around. Had anyone seen me?

No one was running out of the house a couple of hundred yards away. The lights were on, but I saw no activity. The highway was otherwise unoccupied. I had been the lone vehicle on that stretch of the road, and still was.

I restarted the engine. I could tell one of the headlights was shorted out. It was dark. I could not tell where my entry point in the fence was. It was a straight shot from where I sat to the road. I gunned it.

Through the fence I went. Sparks flew in the rain in front of me as I broke through, I kept driving until I hit the highway, and then I kept going without looking back. From time to time, I reflect on that event and realize how God has protected me and delivered me from the shameful wreck I was. And the fool I was needed His protection.

It wasn't long after that when things got tough for me financially. My delivery job with Aetna had come to an end. I was running around with DeWayne, pretending to be entrepreneurial. He had started a nonprofit association, and I found myself helping him get it off the ground. The more I helped, the more he asked from me. Soon, I found myself putting all my energy into that and not making money through other channels.

I made it easy for him to manipulate me. He'd keep me motivated with empty promises in the same way he manipulated his girlfriends.

"When this catches on, Allen, we're going to be heroes," he'd say. "Thousands of nurse's aides across Texas will flock to join us. You can write your own ticket."

It sounded good. I had no prospects for a career after college. I didn't know what I was going to do. I was beginning to consider an MFA program, but I wasn't sure I wanted to go out of state. At the time, Iowa Writers' Workshop had the most prestigious and respected creative writing program anywhere in the country. I had the chops. But I was having fun running around with DeWayne. He hooked me up with a couple of married ladies. And I allowed myself to be sidetracked with his promises of glory at starting something new that would help a lot of people. It never happened.

The shoe finally dropped.

When I couldn't pay my rent anymore, I found myself couch surfing. I skipped out on an apartment I was living in one day and DeWayne would talk people into letting me sleep on their sofa for a few days. In some cases, it would be whatever woman he was bagging that week. One woman was a neurolinguistic programmer who made money "counseling" people. She had a spare bedroom for me, but I had to sleep on the floor because there was no bed. She had a teenage son living with her, and she and DeWayne would get into silly psychological games with each other. It felt awkward being around them.

When I got tired of living that way, I told DeWayne I wasn't helping him with his nonprofit association anymore, and I found a job.

Working for others had the same effect on me as being in a relationship. I had no freedom. I worked fast food for a while, and then tried my hand at a convenience store before drifting into a liquor store one day and applying for a store clerk's position. That was the best part-time job I had after the delivery driver gig. But I was still someone else's employee, and the money wasn't great. It paid for my recreational activities. That was it.

Eventually, I'd tire of juggling schoolwork with employment. I found that employers didn't want to work around my course schedule. And that's when I had the spiritual breakdown. I finished my class assignment on time and dropped it off at the professor's office. It wasn't writing I was proud of, but it was sufficient to complete the course.

The assignment was to defend a philosophy we had discussed in class that semester. Since the professor had discussed Christianity, and God had since proven to me that He is real, I wrote an essay stating why I believed Christianity to be true. I was not well-versed in the Bible at that time, so it wasn't a great essay. I felt like if I got a failing grade on the essay, I'd end the class with a C since everything else I had done to that point had earned an A. Instead, the professor failed me for the course. It was the first failing grade I'd ever received.

I had a right to challenge the grade, but I was spiritually weak and emotionally beaten. Instead, I got on with life. A constant tugging in my spirit told me I was on a different path than the one I was used to. God was leading me somewhere.

Discussion Questions

1) How would you describe the author's spiritual condition during this period of his life?

2) Who, or what, would you say was his god? What were his objects of worship?

3) What could he have done to be happier and more fulfilled?

4) If you were this young man and you could change one thing about yourself, what would it be?

5) What evidence can you see in this story of a young man reaping what he sowed?

6) Can you relate to any parts of his story?

PART 3

Instinctively, I knew I needed a church. It was not something I had to be taught. The Holy Spirit living within me, the one who had poured himself out on me upon my request, implanted the knowledge in my head that surrounding myself with other believers was a necessity. That instinct also informed me that the toxic environment of my childhood was not the right environment for me. So where then?

It wasn't a full week before a knock on my door led me down a path from which there'd be no return.

I had committed myself to finding a church to attend the next Sunday. I don't remember the day of the week of my "upper room" experience, but it was just a couple of days before a knock on my door interrupted my regular routine. I believe it was a Thursday or Friday evening.

I opened the door. Standing before me was a chisel-faced man sporting a tie and holding a Bible in one hand, a plain-dressed woman whose smile enhanced her plainness with a natural glory that appeared to jump off a painter's canvas, and, between them, a cute little girl wearing a paisley dress. The man introduced himself as the pastor of a new church that was meeting at a hotel up the street. They called themselves The New Testament Church.

I invited them in.

There wasn't much furniture. I was a bachelor, a loner, living in an efficiency apartment. The man sat on the sofa, giving his wife room to plant herself. She slid in on one side of him and pulled their daughter to her lap. I sat on the opposite side of the preacher.

He shared a few Bible verses with me, and I told him my story, including the strange experience with the Holy Spirit that had happened a few days before.

"Praise God!" he exclaimed.

His wife, demure as a newborn kitten, said something unmemorable.

I decided to give their church a shot. The following Sunday, still uncertain whether my meeting this family was a divine appointment, I found myself sitting in a chair in a small hotel conference room. There was another couple, a black couple, also in attendance. That caught my attention because Dallas wasn't known for its racial integration, even on Sunday mornings.

They were nice folks. Friendly, smiling, humble, and focused on planting their church.

A week or two later, a young couple and a male friend of theirs joined us. They had moved recently from Maryland and lived in an apartment complex down the street from me. We quickly became friends and I visited them in their home a couple of times a week. One Sunday morning, however, I noticed their absence.

The pastor had been meeting with them, as he was with me in my home, to discuss the Bible. He'd stop by on a weeknight and read a few verses and talk about what they meant. He didn't know I had grown up reading the King James Bible, so I didn't agree with his interpretation of every verse. I didn't want to make waves, so I listened as he talked. When he'd leave, I'd pull out my Bible, ask God to reveal to me what He wanted me to know, and I'd study on my own.

One evening, I walked down the street and knocked on my new friends' door. I don't remember either of the couple's names, but their friend's name was John Fernandes. John answered.

They invited me in. After a few minutes of small talk, they told me that they wouldn't be going back to The New Testament Church.

"Why not?" I asked, a bit curious.

The husband, I'll call him Chris, passing a furtive glance toward his wife, said, "We have a few doctrinal differences."

"Oh."

John chuckled.

I didn't press the issue, but the incident did set me on the path to questioning why the Christian church is so full of "doctrinal differences." It was none of my business why they felt that church wasn't for them, but Chris continued. "The pastor stopped by this week, and we had an interesting discussion."

That piqued my interest. "Yeah?"

"He told us it was a sin for Sue to wear makeup." He glanced at Sue, who smirked and rolled her eyes. "After that," Chris laughed, "we were like, uh, we're outta here!"

I didn't blame him. I couldn't find anything in the Bible that prohibited makeup either. But it did make me think of the good old days of growing up in The Church by Christ Jesus, my mom's church. Mom had instructed my sisters and me to dress plainly and not wear anything on our faces that would draw attention to ourselves. Like makeup. It was of the devil.

Mom never wore it. And Dad had a psychological aversion to it. A family legend I'd heard him tell a few times involved his mother getting upset at Granddad on one occasion and powdering her face with makeup. She was planning to leave him. But she didn't. They remained married until Granddad passed away while I was in the Army. He pastored a small Pentecostal church in southern Louisiana for many years.

While the rules had been loosened in recent years, there were still members of my Mom's denomination who were adamantly opposed to women wearing makeup, cutting their hair, and wearing pants. Those things did not please God, they believed.

I didn't want to spend my first few weeks as a Christian wrangling over rules of legality. I understood where Chris was coming from, but I didn't engage them on it. But what he said next took me by surprise.

"We're not saying you shouldn't go to that church if you feel that's where God is leading you," he said. "But we're not going back."

I had not said one way or another whether I intended to go back to The New Testament Church. At the time, I did believe that's where God wanted me, but I didn't know why. I felt it in my spirit. That's where He wanted me to be.

Sue was not caked with makeup. She used it so modestly that it was barely noticeable, but it was noticeable if you were looking for it. It didn't bother me.

The next Sunday, I went to the church at the hotel as I had done the previous three or four weeks. Everything seemed normal at first. I arrived, shook everyone's hand. They were all smiles and asked how my week went. Cordial and friendly. Small talk. And there were a couple subtle hints about separating myself from those who walked with the devil. I ignored them. A few minutes passed and the service began.

Then things got weird.

We opened our hymnals and began to sing. I don't remember if this happened on the first hymn or the second, but not long into the praise and worship, the pastor, who lead the hymn singing, raised his hands in the air and ordered, "Saints, pray in tongues."

Immediately, the pastor and his wife, and the other couple, began to babble. I looked around and all hands were in the air, waving and flaying, as "the saints" red-facedly prayed their way into God's glory. A prodding of the Holy Spirit made me realize this was a false spirit, not the real deal. I looked curiously at the pastor at the front of the conference room. His hands still raised, he glared at me as if to say, *you are not one of us.* We made eye contact and I knew that I wasn't.

I felt like walking out of the service right then. But I didn't. I waited around, listened to the sermon, and reflected on what had just happened. When I left, I went straight to Chris's and Sue's house.

Surprisingly, they were home.

"We found a church," Chris said.

"Awesome. Where?"

"It's in Irving."

Irving was about a half hour drive from where we lived in North Dallas. I thought, *you couldn't find a church closer to where you live?* I said, "Did you go there today?"

"No," Chris said. "But we called them. They seem like nice people. We're going to try them out next week."

"It's a Nazarene church," John added.

I didn't know what a Nazarene church was, but I congratulated them on finding a church and then told them what happened at the hotel. They all looked at each other as if they had known that might happen.

"That doesn't surprise me," Sue said, walking into the kitchen. She stuck her head around the corner and looked at me. "We were about to eat lunch. Want to join us?"

Over lunch, we discussed different kinds of churches and something about the Bible. I found that they had about as much Bible knowledge as the average Christian does. They weren't scholars, but they understood God's grace. And they were committed to the pop rock culture of contemporary Christianity. Chris was a band manager for a couple of Christian rock bands and would do his work in the evenings. Having been sheltered from all of that growing up, I had no clue. I couldn't be against it, but I found it strange.

"You're welcome to go to church with us next week," Chris said.

"Sure, I'd like that."

I could still feel the tug of the Holy Spirit pulling me toward some unknown distance. I was skeptical of everything. Thumbing through the phone book, I could see all kinds of denominations, each with its own unique take on the gospel, each emphasizing its own set of doctrinal understandings. And the church of my upbringing was just one of the options. I found it all confusing. Which church is the right church? The Spirit inside me told me there was no right church. *Follow me.*

I followed, but I wondered where God was leading me, and why.

At that time, I had no car. My life was in God's hand. Until then, I was used to running the show. I had a vehicle, I had a job, I had a place to live, I had a dream, and I had the plan. It was a loose plan, but it was a plan. It was *my plan.* Suddenly, I had no control over my circumstances. I had control over how I responded to situations, but in the late twentieth century, to be without a vehicle meant a lot less control and a lot more reliance on the mercy of God. It was foreign to me to live that way.

But I was hungry. Spiritually. And I knew I needed the fellowship of other believers. Real believers. A group of Christians who could encourage me and nurture me. I didn't know where to look. I simply followed the Spirit.

When I walked into the Nazarene Church, I felt the grace of God. There was no condemnation, and they stressed that point at every turn.

The people were nice, they were friendly, and they loved Jesus. The services were uplifting, and the pastor was articulate. It was also much bigger than what I was used to. Several hundred people filed into the sanctuary to worship God and listen to the pastor deliver his Sunday sermons. And they had more than one service.

While I enjoyed the services and the people at that church, I knew it wasn't for me. Something was a little bit off even if I couldn't place it. Nevertheless, I attended with my friends for a few weeks, until I could afford to buy a car.

One thing that tipped me off was a praise and worship session one Sunday morning. I looked up and saw the associate pastor with his arms raised high and his face red as the sun. It didn't look natural. It didn't appear spiritual. I got the sense that he was worshiping in the flesh, and I didn't particularly sense that the church leadership was in tune with the Spirit of God. There was something shallow, superficial about it all.

Another thing that rubbed me the wrong way was the pastor parading a group of political candidates across the stage one Sunday and introducing them. It came awfully close to an endorsement in my mind, which didn't seem appropriate.

I wasn't concerned about the legality of it. It didn't seem right to interrupt worship to inform the congregation that "Christian" candidates were available for their votes. They could have been faithful Christians and may have stood for all the right values. Who knows? I may have agreed with them on some of their political talking points, but that was not the right venue for politics. I knew that instinctively.

That was the only time I've ever seen that happen. Although, I have been in churches where the pastor has honored a political candidate, or office holder, by announcing their presence. It always rubs me the wrong way. Over the years, I've grown very sensitive to it, and I've noticed it takes place more often during election years. I do not even like walking into a church and seeing an American flag at the front of the sanctuary. It's not that I believe there is anything sacred about the building, but there is something sacred about God's people worshiping together, and I don't want to be distracted by the vision of this world's national and cultural icons while I'm trying to worship God.

On a positive note, it was at that large Nazarene church where I learned about the blessing, when believers lift their hands and aim their palms at another as someone prays. I've read the Bible through the years, but I've never found anything that supports that practice. Of course, I haven't read anything that condemns it either. So I don't pass judgment. However, it does illustrate to me the vast diversity of expression that God has in His church.

I moved in with Chris, Sue, and John at one point for a few months. Working at Time-Life Libraries and living with them allowed me to save money to buy a car. But I was a lousy salesman.

At the time, Time-Life had a ten-week training program for new sales reps. They paid a minimum wage, or commissions. If commissions didn't exceed one's wage earnings for a twenty-five-hour work week, the trainee was let go after ten weeks. We worked in four-hour shifts, and there were three shifts each day, plus a five-hour shift on Saturdays. If a rep wanted to work more than twenty-five hours a week, he could work on one of the other shifts, but only on a straight-commission basis.

Since I didn't have a car when I started at Time-Life, I rode the bus to work each day. I really wanted to succeed, but I pushed myself too hard. I had not learned yet to rest in God's grace. As a result, my own mental anguish at trying to perform came through in my voice when on the phone with prospects. I sounded hostile. Entering the tenth week, the Dallas branch manager called me into his office. John Penderton was his name.

"Allen, how do you feel you're doing?"

"Not well." I felt deflated.

"You're making some sales, but you're not hitting the minimums. Is the training helping you?"

I told him I was trying to do my best.

"I see." John had an unnaturally baritone voice. It was well-trained and designed to make him sound authoritative. He had been an actor before joining Time-Life about two decades earlier. "You know, at the end of the week, if you're not hitting the numbers, we'll have to let you go."

"I'll do it! I'll hit the numbers."

"It sounds like you're under a lot of stress," John said. He played a recording of one of my calls for me so I could hear myself. They recorded all the calls of trainees to use for training purposes and would use those to coach us throughout the ten-week training period. I listened to the recording. I could hear the stress. "You got a lot going on right now?"

I didn't expect it to get personal. Taken aback, I responded, somewhat ashamed, "I don't have a car right now," I said. "I need to make enough money for a car. And rent."

If I could have looked in a mirror, I'm sure I'd have seen a load of sadness in my eyes. And probably some guilt. I was not taking failure very well.

"I'd like to make you an offer." My ears perked up. "We have an opening in the lead sorting department. It pays minimum wage, but you'll work a full eight hours every day. You can start right now."

I took a deep breath. I knew I'd make a lot more money if I could figure out how to sell. I also knew that people skills did not come naturally to me. I was struggling, and it wasn't likely to change. John knew that. I didn't. "I'd really like to stay on the sales floor," I said.

It was hardly a sales floor. It was a boiler room. About thirty fast talkers sat in one big room, desks in a row, microphones on their heads, each trying to persuade the person on the other end of the phone to listen, stay tuned in, and whip out their credit card. Some of the salespeople made it look natural. It was not natural to me.

John looked at me with empathy. "Okay," he said, leaning back in his huge executive chair. "But at the end of the week, if you don't hit your numbers, I'll have to let you go."

"I understand," I said, then I went back to my desk to fail some more.

When my shift was over, my supervisor, a buxom and vivacious older woman named Carol, caught me on my way out the door. She was built like a feminine linebacker and looked like she wanted to tackle me.

"Allen," she said, with all the confidence I wished I could have mustered, "I heard you turned down the lead sorting job."

Seriously? These people were sure taking an interest in me. I wasn't used to that at all. I didn't know what to do. I wanted to succeed, at something. And that job was my best opportunity. Reluctantly, I said, "Yeah. I–"

"I think you should take the job," she said. "It would really help you."

The huge smile on her face was as unnatural as John's voice, but I could tell she was trying to help me. And I knew taking that job was the right thing, even though it wasn't what I wanted.

There was not a hint of a Christian spirit anywhere at Time-Life. It was a bastion of political liberalism. But I also felt like God was taking care of me. He wasn't using my family, the Bible, the church, or anything remotely resembling Christ to do it. He was using the pagan, worldly system to shower me with His love, and to work out the details of my life in a way that I could not.

"I'll think about it," I said. And I did. I went home, got on my knees, prayed to God, read some Bible verses, and nurtured myself to sleep. The next morning, I got up, prayed, read the Bible some more, and thought about John's offer. The Spirit within me prodded me to take it. It was the right thing to do, and I knew it. But I also couldn't see how making a minimum wage was going to help me earn the money I needed to buy a vehicle and pay my rent and utility bills, plus food. When it was time, I walked to the bus stop and went to work. I walked into the office, went straight to John's office door, and knocked.

"Come in!" I entered and told John that I'd like the job in the lead sorting department. "Great! Want to start right now?"

I didn't. "Sure." And right away, he led me to the lead sorting department to introduce me to my new co-worker.

Danny was a red-faced red-headed Irish homosexual, as open as a gay man could be. If he hadn't openly admitted it, I'd have known for sure just by his mannerisms. We never talked about it. I didn't try to tell him he was an awful sinner, and he didn't try to get into my pants. We had a good working relationship for the six months I worked in the department. He trained me on the simple tasks of the job, and I was able to buy a vehicle after a couple of months. Of course, by then, I was living with Chris, Sue, and John, sleeping on the floor in John's bedroom.

It was easy work. Our job was to sort leads by the various types and put them all in boxes according to the type of lead they were.

The leads were thin sheets of paper, approximately three inches by six inches, with typewritten contact information of potential product buyers. There were two primary categories: Previous customers and people who had never bought from Time-Life. The previous customers were subcategorized into the types of products they had purchased in the past. The best leads, previous customers, were reserved for the best sales reps. Trainees were given the "cold" leads, people who had never purchased a Time-Life product before. If you wanted to get the best leads, you had to prove yourself.

Working in the lead department gave me a different perspective on the sales process. I was able to break it down and see that there were essentially three types of customers. There were those who were not familiar with Time-Life products, those who had purchased one or a part of a series in the past, and those who had purchased multiple product series and were product evangelists. They were easy to sell to.

One day, executives from the corporate office came in and met with John behind his closed office door. They were there for most of the day, and John spent a lot of time walking out of the office, coming into the lead sorting room, grabbing a box off the top shelf of an area I didn't spend much time interacting with, and going back to his office. At the end of the day, one of the bigwigs from the corporate office shut down all the phones and addressed everyone who was there. John had left the building.

Danny and I joined the rest of the staff on the sales floor and listened to the stuffed shirt in front of us explain that John was let go and they'd bring us another branch manager as soon as they could. A few days later, a tall mustachioed bag of cockiness from Seattle introduced himself as our new manager.

Mike Snodgrass was not well liked. Unlike John Penderton, he was not personable, diplomatic, or empathetic. But he gave me a second chance.

With business-like precision, he jumped in with both feet. He called every employee, one by one, into his office and asked each of us what we'd like to see happen. What improvements we'd like to see made, where we see ourselves being in a year or two, and what we'd like to do next. When he called me into his office, I told him I wanted to go back on the sales floor.

"You were on the sales floor?" he asked.

"Yeah, I went through the training, but I wasn't good at it. I had a lot going on and was under a lot of stress. I guess it came through on the phone because I just couldn't get the hang of it. I think I can do it now."

Life was different at that time. I had a car, my financial situation wasn't as bleak as it had been before, I had spent a lot of time praying and studying my Bible, and I had found another church where I could worship with God's people and experience His grace. I was happy, and relaxed.

"Okay then," Mike said. "I'll see what I can do about that."

A few days later, I found myself on the sales floor again. This time, my supervisor was a black woman named Cecilia. She was a great supervisor. I found her very encouraging, a great coach, and easy to open up to. She likewise took a liking to me.

I knew the people at Time-Life liked me, but I also knew they saw me as a strange kid with odd ideas. I befriended a mixed-race older man named Curtis Joe. I never asked him his background, but he looked albino, had a black and orange pigmentation and reddish-orange hair. It made him interesting to me. He was a smart guy. Different, but very liberal.

One day, between shifts, Curtis and I sat in the break room together and he asked me about my faith. Word had got out that I was a Christian. I didn't wear it on my sleeve, but I didn't stuff it in my pocket either.

"How did you come to believe?" He asked.

I shared my story, then he shared his. I could tell he wasn't a Christian, but he believed in God. As he shared his story, I sensed a deep reflection about the things of life. He shared with me a time when he almost drowned and called out to God for help. Suddenly, he said, a hand reached down and grabbed him, pulled him up to the surface of the water, and pulled him into a boat. He also said something about a vision of an angel, a white light, or something, that he had while under the water.

That's interesting, I thought. But how do you question that? Maybe it was an angel. Maybe it was Christ. Maybe it was an overactive imagination. Whatever it was, it had an impact on Curtis Joe. He had his story, I had mine.

Not long after that, I went into work one day and was met with the assistant branch manager, a short stocky man named Dan. He stood about five feet two. And broad-shouldered. He wasn't fat, he was lean, but he looked like he could have been a circus performer with his handlebar mustache, and he was a stellar sales pro. He could talk people into giving up their credit card information in a heartbeat. He stopped me on my way into the building and said the office was closed for the day. Shut down.

"What?"

I couldn't believe it. Who shuts down a sales floor? This had to be a joke, but Dan wasn't laughing.

"Someone pulled a gun on Mike," he said.

Whoa! "Are you kidding?"

"No." He told me who. It didn't surprise me. Mike wasn't known for his diplomacy. If he had something to say, he said it. And it didn't matter how it sounded. The man Dan said had pulled the gun was involved in selling drugs.

By that time, I had gone through my second ten-week training period and was rocking the sales floor. I rose to being one of the top salespeople on my shift, and they were grooming me for a shift supervisor position. I found it surprising how easy it was to sell to some people. I had done so well that I was allowed to work the easy leads. These were people who had purchased multiple Time-Life products in the past. There were people who, as soon as I mentioned Time-Life, said, "What have you got this time? I'd tell them and they'd say, "Sign me up!"

I learned to modify my sales script with these people. It was a truncated sales pitch, designed to get to the call to action quicker. And it worked.

Being a shift supervisor would have involved training others, evaluating their performance, and motivating the sales reps with prizes for performance. It also would have involved tracking production on the big whiteboard at the front of the boiler room. I got a chance to do it a few times as they were grooming me for that position, but before that process could be consummated the corporate office announced they were closing the Dallas sales office. We were all soon to be out of a job.

During this time, I attended a nondenominational church called Hillcrest Church. After I bought my vehicle, I started looking for a church closer to where I lived. I found Hillcrest Church, named for the street that it was on. The pastor was a man named Dr. Morris Sheats. I loved his preaching. I found it to be practical, and it spoke to where I was at in my life.

One of the things that stuck with me about Pastor Morris is the way he applied scripture to practical everyday living. To this day, after twenty-eight years of listening to sermons, one of the most memorable ones was a sermon by Dr. Sheats.

I don't remember the entire sermon. What I remember is his exhortation to develop a philosophy of failure. In fact, that was the name of his sermon—A Philosophy of Failure.

At one point during his sermon, he said, "You've got to develop a philosophy of failure for your life." That has stuck with me all these years because, at that time, failure was precisely the thing I was dealing with. Going through the financial troubles I went through, due to my own bad decision-making, caused me to think about it a lot. What causes it? Why does it happen? What should a Christian do when it happens? And I developed a philosophy of failure.

I also immersed myself in a small group fellowship at Hillcrest Church and joined the singles group. All my spare time was spent independently studying the Bible. I was hungry and fed on God's word every chance I could get. Where before, while in college, I'd spend hours writing, I suddenly found myself spending the same amount of time studying the Bible. Day in, day out. It became my passion.

There was also a home group nearby that met once a week, and I got involved in it. A friend of mine from Hillcrest Church invited me one night. It was like a church service. Every Thursday night, about fifty people mingled over a huge buffet of food before gathering for worship. We spent a good deal of time singing praise songs before a Bible study.

The man who ran the group, and in whose home, we met, was a recovered alcoholic. Many of the other participants were also recovering alcoholics, but there were many who just came for the worship. It was a rich experience and taught me more about God's diversity.

One Sunday morning, during worship at Hillcrest Church, I was taken by surprise when the gentleman standing next to me turned and said, "I can see the Lord's anointing on you."

"Really?"

He was a salesman by trade, a smooth-faced man not much older than me, but he told me he had the gift of discernment and could see God's anointing all over me. How he could see that just from standing beside me for a few minutes was beyond me. But it drove me to the Bible. What did it have to say about discernment? I learned about spiritual gifts and began to take an interest in them. I wondered what my gifts were. How would I know?

Every time I heard something I couldn't get my mind around; I ran to the Bible. I read up on it. I studied it. I meditated. I prayed God would give me understanding. I thirsted after God's own heart.

Two books that challenged me were Romans and Ephesians. The entire New Testament spurred me on, but I liked Romans because it gave me a lot to think about. It read like a philosophical treatise, and that appealed to my mind. Having read a lot of philosophy, the brainy concepts in Romans made me think of life through a different lens. I soaked it in.

Romans 8 flabbergasted me. That there is no condemnation for those in Christ Jesus, which I was, washed over me like bath water. It cleansed me of all my guilt. Verses twenty-eight through thirty became my go-to passages in times of trouble. When I'd experience doubt, fear, anxiety, shame, or anything that led me away from God's love, I'd remind myself of these verses. Sometimes, it was daily. Eventually, I'd grow to not need the injection as frequently, but I went back to those verses over and over to remind myself of the depth of God's love for me. They also told me that He is the master of my life; I am not.

Ephesians gave me a broad and beautiful view of the church. Twenty-eight years later, I'm still mesmerized by the picture it gives of the body of Christ.

These two books pushed me toward a Reformed understanding of scripture. I could not get my head wrapped around a God who predestinated His future creation, but there it was in plain black and white. How could I deny it? God knew me before the foundation of the world. And He called me out of my spiritual deadliness to be a light amid the darkness. Not just me, but His entire church, the mystery of all mysteries. Over the years, as I've gone back to Ephesians, I've been just as mesmerized that the church today is no closer to resembling that image of Christ's bride as it ever was. The fragmented nature of the church, with its many denominations and competing doctrines, looks nothing like that which was conceived in eternity past, and which exists in the bosom of God's eternal purpose.

At least, it looks nothing like that from my vantage point. Yet, I've wondered what it looks like from God's vantage point. I am humbled to say that I am in no position to judge.

I met some great people at Hillcrest Church. I learned about God's grace and just how low it will steep to scoop up the most awful of sinners, of which I was one. But no matter how hard I tried; I could not stop sinning. I still had some fleshly desires pulling at me. Quite often, I'd give in. Over time, I'd find myself giving in much less often, but my conscience kept me focused on the "unsearchable riches of Christ" the Apostle Paul alluded to in Ephesians 3:8.

The small group I participated in met in a married couple's home, but most of us were singles. We all became good friends. The group consisted of a young single woman named Carla Sprinkles, a black man named Wilten Haynes who, I learned, was no fan of Hootie and the Blowfish lead singer Darius Rucker, and John Fernandes. John and I had moved in together and were roommates in a two-bedroom apartment, a step up for both of us.

When John became unemployed at one point, I helped him write a resumé and he ended up working as a tech support specialist at Microsoft. He made sure I kept myself clean of sexual immorality.

One night, in a small group meeting, I mentioned that I wanted to destroy some icons from my past.

"I have a lot of poems and stories I've written over the years," I said. "I'd like to burn them."

The members of the group were supportive, but none of them asked me why I wanted to do that. No one bothered asking, "Do you think it will make you a better Christian, or earn you favor with God?"

I did not believe that it would do either of those things. I simply wanted to get rid of these personal reminders of the kind of person I was so that I could focus on the type of person I was becoming. It was a noble sentiment, but biblically unsound. I was still not resting in God's grace.

One of those poems was "Threesome." It had not been published, but only because I never sent it to a publisher. I'm confident that, had I done so, it would have seen the light of day. I wanted to rid myself of the temptation.

When we had our next meeting, I brought reams of notebooks and folders full of poems and fiction I had written. They were not all bad. Some were quite good. That is, they were excellent literary pieces and could not be construed as obscene or otherwise reflective of a devilish worldview. They weren't Christian in any sense, but at that time in my life I had not considered what it means to honor God with one's creative craft.

It didn't take long to discover that the circle of people I had surrounded myself by were conservative in their politics, and it seemed that there was an expectation that a Christian would lean conservative politically. Many of them were Rush Limbaugh fans.

I was not.

There was nothing about Rush Limbaugh that I found to be offensive, particularly, nor was there anything I found particularly attractive. I mean this in a philosophical sense. To me, he was a radio commentator with a conservative-leaning political philosophy, but he didn't seem to be coming from a Christian worldview. I asked my small group one evening, "Why do so many Christians like Rush Limbaugh?"

The married gentleman in the group, in whose house we met, was quick to answer. "Because he's conservative."

Over the years, I've contemplated the conservative-liberal divide within the church and have found myself disappointed that Christians of both persuasions so easily cast aspersions on each other with *ad hominem* attacks and misapplications of scripture in order to rationalize their own attachment to the icons of this world while rejecting the clear New Testament exhortation to seek unity in Christ. And it's gotten worse. I found myself studying political philosophy a little more deeply to try and understand where these mostly well-meaning people are coming from. At one point, I drifted toward libertarianism because I couldn't identify with either Republicans or Democrats.

I couldn't justify my political philosophy with scripture, and I didn't try. In my mind, the United States is as much under the control of the "god of this world" as every other nation. My citizenship is in heaven. I'm a stranger and an alien on this planet, in this realm. And to this day I am embarrassed for Christ when someone uses God, the Bible, or Jesus to justify their harsh rhetoric of someone with whom they disagree politically.

When Time-Life re-opened its Dallas office after the gun incident, they brought in recruiters from other telemarketing firms to interview those of us who wanted to seek employment. I met with a couple of men who worked at Fenton Swanger, a consumer research firm with a telemarketing division.

"Division" is an overstatement. It was a small company, and both the consumer research and telemarketing teams worked in one boiler room, which was considerably smaller than the boiler room at Time-Life. But they knew what they were doing.

The company was run by women. All the lead executives in the company, except one, were female. They had a unique niche. They contracted with companies to call people and businesses and conduct telephone surveys. In their telemarketing division, they'd contract with companies to sell products, set appointments, generate and qualify leads, and a host of other services related to telemarketing and telesales. We worked on a per-project basis, so I'd find myself doing something different from week to week. We were paid an hourly wage plus bonuses, depending on the assignment. I liked it.

While at Fenton Swanger, I got the opportunity to write a few scripts for the telemarketing team, which I enjoyed, and I supervised a few of the projects. In all, it was a great experience, but I wasn't satisfied. Something was missing.

The truth is, I still had some worldly habits to overcome. Despite the time I spent in Bible study and prayer, I still fought my fleshly desires.

I worked at Fenton Swanger for a little over a year. One of the co-workers was an attractive lady who took an interest in me. I asked her out and we went to dinner and a movie. She brought a friend. I thought it was strange at the time, but I realized later it was her way of protecting herself. And she wanted to get her girlfriend's input on me.

After dinner, her friend left. My date and I went to a movie. Afterwards, we stood at her vehicle and talked. I tried to be a gentleman. The conversation turned to where to go from here.

"I used to be involved in the swinging lifestyle," she divulged to me. She was testing me, wanting to see my reaction.

I debated whether I should tell her I had too. I chose not to. Instead, tempted as I was to make a move, I told her I enjoyed the date but that we should probably not move forward. We weren't going to be each other's type. As much as I wanted to take her home, I knew it wasn't right. We worked together for a few more weeks before she went on to another job.

Another woman at Fenton Swanger threw a picture of herself in my face one day. She was the phone receptionist in the telemarketing section and performed some administrative tasks for the office. I had just dialed a number, and someone had answered on the other end. I was about to start talking when the receptionist turned around and shoved a picture in my face. "See my tattoo?" she teased.

I was gob smacked.

Two inches from my face was this Polaroid image of my co-worker lying naked on a bed. She had a tattoo of a flower on her pelvis. She had placed her thumb just right so that I couldn't see anything but the tattoo, her legs spread at a forty-five-degree angle, and her belly. Despite having been a heroin addict before getting clean, she was knock-down gorgeous, and I had contemplated asking her for a date. My heart racing, I hung up the phone and clutched the cubicle wall next to me. I had to excuse myself to run down the hall and get a drink of water. My mouth had gone dry.

When I returned, she was at her desk piddling with her paperwork. Everyone else was on the phone making calls. One co-worker, a married woman named Marlene, looked at me as if wondering what I'd do next. She could see I was struggling.

"Wow!" I said and went back to work.

There was temptation at every corner. It wasn't all sexual. Sometimes, it was somebody, or some event, testing the limits of my patience. Like Dad, I could rage at the drop of a hat. I found that I could take all of these temptations to God in prayer, and they'd subside. He could deal with them; I could not.

One day, I walked into a Joshua's Christian Bookstore and saw a notice on the front door that they were looking for store managers. I applied for the position and got the job. After a couple of months training with one of their store managers, a personable Christian gentleman named Rob Schumacher, I was to open my own store.

It proved to be a fatal mistake, but quite the learning experience.

The day before I was to report for my store opening, the chain's regional manager invited me to his office. It didn't sound like an invitation. It was my day off, and he knew it. He wanted me to drive to his office on my day off to, essentially, "feel me out." That was about all I could gather from that meeting.

I'd been a Christian for, maybe, three years at that point. I'd struggled financially and emotionally, and I'd learned to overcome sexual temptation. But I was still dealing with the psychological funk of legalism and fatherly despotism. I was browbeaten and still recovering.

As it were, I didn't have the confidence to say, "Hey, that's my day off. Can we do it the next day?" Instead, I agreed to the meeting and showed up in jeans and a button-down shirt. That was an idiot move. To top it off, I was about five minutes late because I had trouble finding a parking space. My boss's office was tucked off in a corner of a building, which was situated out of the way of major traffic arteries. It was a small company, so they couldn't afford the luxury of Taj Mahal office spaces.

After a couple of minutes of uncomfortable small talk, Steve made a passing remark about me being "fashionably late." He couched it in a comment to his assistant sitting at her desk a few feet away, but I knew what he was getting at. I felt like a vassal.

Then he wanted to know what my background was. I didn't feel comfortable sharing that. What should I say? I couldn't say I'd grown up in a legalistic environment (I wasn't familiar with that term yet). I was attending a nondenominational church, and I wasn't familiar with that many denominations at that time anyway. It was something I'd just have soon not known about.

"I go to a church called Hillcrest Church," I said, with consternation.

Steve wore a white shirt. A tie. He could have been more conservative than Rush Limbaugh.

"I'm Presbyterian. PCA."

I had no idea what that meant.

"I'm not familiar with that," I said, still uncomfortable. Steve had a sort of confidence that seemed unnatural. He was confident in all the wrong things—his denomination, his doctrine, his position.

"We're the conservative ones," he said. "The PCUSA think we're heathens. We think they're heathens." He smiled.

I really didn't care. I gathered he was half-joking.

The purpose for that meeting was simply to let me know we were getting started on the track to opening a new store in Fort Worth and I was going to be its manager. It sounded good, but I wasn't ready. There were parts of my life I had not surrendered to God, but I wasn't aware of it consciously yet. I was walking in the flesh. And Steve didn't help.

Becoming a bookstore manager was a complete life change for me. Opening a store in Fort Worth meant moving from North Dallas to somewhere closer to Fort Worth. Otherwise, it was going to be a long commute each day, nearly an hour one way. After church one Sunday, I bumped into Dr. Sheats and strolled with him down the walkway from the church's front door to the parking lot.

"Dr. Sheats, I want you to know that I've enjoyed being a part of your church," I said, earnestly.

"Are you leaving?"

"Yessir." I explained that I was taking a new job and it was going to require a move so that I could be closer to work.

"Well, it sounds like a great opportunity. We'll miss you."

"I learned a lot from your preaching."

He thanked me and we parted ways.

I didn't have the sense then to stay in touch with friends after a move. I left Hillcrest Church without exchanging contact information with anyone I had met there. It was not something my parents taught me to do. We hadn't kept in touch with the Leidigs, and after moving to Dallas, the only friends Mom and Dad had, that I was aware of, were the people at church. Mostly family.

So, I said goodbye to Dr. Sheats and moved to Fort Worth. I was completely disconnected.

After moving to Fort Worth, I found another church. Inside the city of Arlington, where the Texas Rangers play, there is a little municipality called Pantego. It had a Bible church.

Pantego Bible Church was pastored by a young sanguine Dallas Theological Seminary graduate named Randy Frazee. He had written a book. He had to be a good pastor, right?

The name of his book was "The Comeback Congregation." Published in 1995, the book details how Pastor Frazee led Pantego Bible Church (PBC) to a renewal after losing over a thousand congregants. He rebuilt the ministry and grew the church again to a respectable size. I became one of its members.

I wasn't interested in Pastor Frazee's book. I was still trying to grow into my faith. His preaching, mainly focused on the shallow doctrines, helped me a little, but what helped more than anything is simply living my life, interacting with other believers, and putting my faith into practice.

At PBC, I bounced back and forth between the young singles group and an older group made up mostly of previously married singles. There were some among that group who had never been married, but they were more mature than the younger group. Plus, I liked the Sunday School teacher, an older man by the name of Larry Long. He was a great teacher and spoke with a lot of passion.

Larry would take a passage of scripture and give it real practical application, often sharing when he used it in his own life. I admired his straightforward style.

In the young adult group, a lot of the younger people were there to find a mate. I wasn't. I was simply enjoying life as a Christian, working at the bookstore, and trying to be faithful. I spent a lot of time trying to avoid temptations. If I found myself in a situation where I might be alone to an attractive single lady, I avoided it. Before coming to Christ, I found it difficult to trust others. After coming to Christ, I found it difficult to trust myself.

I also tried to avoid discussions that might get my dander up. Political discussions were often the ones where I found that people would dig their heels in the most to defend their convictions. I didn't want to put myself, or anyone else, in that position, so if a discussion turned to politics, I walked away.

It became even more clear to me that the expectation was for a Christian to lean conservatively. I certainly did in some ways. In others, I didn't.

There was one young lady, a young single mother, who came into Sunday school one morning speaking out against the Harry Potter novels. One thing she said intrigued me. "They teach children witchcraft."

"They do?" I asked.

I had no interest in them since I didn't have children. But she looked at me and said, "Yeah, they're not right. You know better than that."

That did it. I went and bought the first book in the Harry Potter series just to see what she was talking about. I found no recipes for magic. And while I was a little bit concerned about the use of the word "scalawag" for a book aimed at tweens, I thought the books were quite entertaining. Not educational, but entertaining. Harmlessly.

When I got married, I shared those novels with my wife's middle child, Leah. She and I went to see all the Harry Potter movies together, and it became our way of bonding.

What bothered me the most about "patriotic" Christians was their insistence that America was founded as a Christian nation and that it should remain so. I couldn't see the evidence. I confess, still today, I don't see the evidence that Thomas Jefferson, James Madison, John Jay, and the rest intended to establish a nation on Christian principles. To be sure, there was a strong Christian influence on the country's founding, but that influence came by way of cultural grassroots practical living. That's why many local laws at the time were based on Bible principles, but the philosophers of the day wanted to craft a republican institution that respected the rights of minority groups. They were dead set against bullish factions. I think they made that clear.

Nevertheless, my Christian friends, at church and beyond, insisted on propping up their "family values" political heroes, many of whom didn't live the values they claimed to espouse, and advocated for the top-down advancement of "Christian" principles. I didn't think it was the government's duty, nor do I now, to dictate whose principals would guide Satan's stronghold. They talked about America as if it was Christ's bride.

I wanted to be faithful to God. I prayed, I studied the Bible, I attended a weekly small group, and was at Sunday worship every week. Was that enough? Was that all there was to the Christian life? The novelty had worn off and reality set in. Many of my biggest struggles had to do with other Christians, not with the world.

Meanwhile, I worked a lot of hours trying to manage my huge bookstore in Fort Worth. It was about three times the size of the average bookstore in the chain. New to retail and new to retail management, I found it a challenge.

I was good at selling Bibles, and I could take care of the financials, but there were some other areas where I struggled, namely, personal interaction with customers and employees. I had difficulty building rapport with employees, with picking the ones with the right temperament for the environment, and with motivating them to be better retail servants. I had to first learn how to be a good servant myself.

When it became evident that the Fort Worth store was too much for me, Steve arranged for me to switch places with one of the other store managers. He moved me to the Arlington store where I'd be closer to church, and I had less to manage.

The Arlington store was more my size, but I still struggled with spiritual immaturity. I had no mentors and didn't know how to approach one. My own fallenness kept erupting into my day, and I found that other Christians were not as near to perfect as I wanted them to be. Besides having to fight my own fallen nature, I found myself attempting to navigate theirs too.

I took great pride in being a Christian bookstore manager. If I'd simply been a bookstore manager, I'd have quit the first week. But being in the Christian environment at least gave me access to good reading material. I found a lot of great theology to delve into.

It didn't help. I learned a lot. And I discovered that knowledge of God doesn't equate with an experience of God. The two do not necessarily go hand in hand. I became a legalist. A doctrinaire.

And a few knowledgeable Christians at PBC assisted me. Some of them were in seminary, teaching me knew theological words, like "soteriology" and "salvific." I could get back into my head again. Was philosophy bad if it was God's philosophy? I didn't think it was.

A small group of single men at PBC developed a keen interest in all things Reformed. I was among them. It helped that Joshua's was owned and managed by men entrenched in Reformed doctrines. Much of the material we sold in the store, aside from the popular titles that sold well, was solidly Reformed in nature. I read all I could. Everything I could get my hands on. I devoured it with a sort of lavishness one might see in the scavenger sort among nature's animal kingdoms.

Interestingly, the music we carried was quite diverse. Some of it reflected Reformed theology, but a lot of the popular music also came from the Charismatic and Pentecostal side of the Christian family. I was exposed to all of it.

I got good at selling Bibles. And I loved it. I'd ask customers what kind of church they attended and ask them what their favorite Bible passages were. I learned that I could tell a lot about their theological leanings if I asked the right questions, and I delighted in finding them the right Bible for their religious system. If they were Reformed, I'd point them toward a study Bible, such as the Geneva Bible, that reflected the doctrinal tenets of that system. If I sensed they were from a Charismatic, Pentecostal, or "Spirit-Filled" background, I'd point them in the direction of the Spirit-Filled Bible, or an equivalent. If they were dispensationalists, I'd recommend the Scofield Bible or the Ryrie Study Bible. But many customers didn't know what the theological leanings of their teachers were, so in those cases I'd point them toward something more generic like the Life Application Bible or the Living Bible. I became the Bible-selling expert and was proud of my ability to put the right Bible into the hands of the right individual. And my bosses noticed it too.

It didn't take me long to increase the sales figures at the Arlington store. I did that by selling more Bibles and teaching my employees how to sell merchandise. We also focused on making attractive product displays, a necessity in the retail environment.

Meanwhile, I took pride in the theological knowledge I was acquiring. I was learning to be a great legalist. My friends and I would pick apart the pastor's messages and try to find the parts that didn't line up perfectly with John Calvin, John McArthur, and Charles Spurgeon. And we'd have our own discussion groups where we'd delve into the many paths of God's sovereignty or the depths of His magnificent love for the elect. We honored God with our lips, but our hearts went on vacation.

It didn't help, too, that I began to feel the pangs of writing welling up in my soul again. I missed the classroom. I missed spilling my guts out on the page. I wanted to experience the joy of creating again. So, I started writing poetry and attending poetry readings around Dallas and Fort Worth, mostly Fort Worth. The Fort Worth literary scene became my running circle, but I kept a foot in God's door.

I got so into the theological discoveries I was making that I decided to attend a weekly Bible study at First Baptist Arlington. It was highly recommended by my friends at PBC.

It was very well organized. Hundreds of people participated. They assigned each participant to a small group of eight to ten members of the same sex. At orientation, we were given a notebook full of homilies and study questions. Each night, we were to study the assigned scriptures and write our answers in the study guide. Then, on the assigned night of discussion, each small group would meet in a classroom at the large church and discuss what they had discovered during their personal Bible study that week.

One fateful evening, my group met and one of the questions was about Jeremiah 1:5. I remarked that I was having trouble wrapping my head around God knowing the prophet Jeremiah before "I formed you in the womb."

An older gentleman, eager to defend God's word and prove himself a faithful servant, snapped, "What about abortion?" He was quick to point out that he was an elder in his church and "I wouldn't dare question God. If He says it, it's true."

That was my first experience in bumping up against the pride of positional eldering in the body of Christ, and I'd learn many more times after that how the organizational structure of the church itself props up human pride. Men are chosen to lead, then they take pride in their position, often going out of their way to defend some imagined slight against God or themselves. I was simply trying to understand God's foreknowledge. To this day, I still don't understand it. That doesn't mean I don't believe in it.

Human pride is a dreadful thing. It typically precedes a fall. And my own pride would take me by surprise not too long after that incident with the elder, proving that no man is immune from its effects.

I was chatting it up with a couple of the young Christians I had hired for the store and said something inappropriate. It wasn't directed at anyone specifically, but it was certainly off-color. Not vulgar, but out of context. As soon as the words flew from my lips, I knew I was in trouble.

We were shooting the breeze between customer rushes, talking about popular music, or something similarly innocuous. Before I knew it, the unthinkable slipped from my lips.

The next day, Steve called. He took me to lunch and asked about the situation. I was honest. He reprimanded me and made me watch a video on sexual harassment. I took note that we carried the name "Christian" on the front of our store, but we treated this incident like it would be treated in any other workplace. Cold and sterile. No redemption, no restoration, no talk of confession, repentance, or forgiveness. Steve had me sign a piece of paper saying he had talked to me, and we had watched a training video together. Then it went into a personnel file. Hardly Psalm 32.

That was my sin we were dealing with. They didn't have any more respect for it than that? The treatment of it has haunted me more in memory than the actual sin.

Years later, after I had long left that employer, I bumped into the young lady who witnessed my indiscretion that day. She stepped into an elevator I already occupied. When she recognized me, she averted her eyes and looked at the floor. I contemplated whether I should apologize to her then and there, but I didn't want it to cause a scene. I didn't want to make her feel any more uncomfortable than I already had. When it was too late, I concluded I should have apologized.

Months later, while reading an industry magazine, an article prompted my response. I wrote a letter to the editor. It was controversial, but it shouldn't have been.

The funny thing is, I addressed something I thought, and still think, should be addressed by Christian businesses. I can't recall the details exactly, but I remember it had to do with running a business and reflecting Christ at the same time. I suggested that employing the principles of Christian living should take precedence. I signed my name but didn't identify myself with any specific brand establishment. As far as readers would know, I was a voice in the wilderness.

Except for those within the same chain. Management went ballistic.

I got a call.

"Did you write that?"

"Well, it has my name on it."

This happened around the same time a larger Christian bookstore chain called Family Bookstores bought Joshua's. They brought in an entirely different management team. Steve was gone and replaced by a group of men from a Charismatic and Pentecostal background. Some of them were from the Assemblies of God. That's immaterial, but it simply illustrated the point that I had made in my letter. Business was more important than the virtues of Christ.

I found myself suddenly removed from management and placed under the tutelage of another store manager at another location for "re-training." For something that had nothing to do with my job. They didn't even have the gall to fire me. Another incident a few weeks later would give impetus for that.

We were asked to print some tickets for an event, and the printer for that exercise was sent to the store where I was being re-trained. I was going to be the one to deliver those tickets to their destination, so I was behind the retail counter babysitting the printer. One of the other employees came over and asked, "What are you doing? What are those for?"

I didn't think it was any of her business, but I didn't think it mattered. "They're for me," I said.

I wasn't being cocky. It was my impersonable demeanor showing up again, and the lack of wisdom in understanding how it might be perceived. She walked away faster than she had appeared. A few minutes later, the regional manager, Steve's replacement, a big fellow from a charismatic background who had been a store manager, came over. He talked to me about the situation and asked me what happened. I told him.

He was gracious and kind, instructing me that I should have just told the girl what we were doing. I agreed. A few days later, executives came down, took me to the manager's office, and told me I was history. Cold, sterile, just like any other workplace.

I didn't understand why my non-Christian employers treated me better than the Christian ones, but I knew God was in control. I wasn't.

It could have embittered me, but I wouldn't let it. I simply moved on. A few days later, I was back in telemarketing. And the friction of my Christian life was chiseling away at the rough edges, sharpening the iron of my dinked armor.

I had also joined the National Guard while managing the Arlington store. I was dating a young lady who was in the Guard at the time. After looking into it myself, I decided to take the plunge. I remembered how much I enjoyed active duty, but that was a full decade earlier. Since I had most of my college completed, if I finished my education, they'd send me to officer candidate school (OCS). I didn't even need to finish college before starting OCS if I completed my education before graduating.

In the meantime, tension was building.

Joni, the woman I was dating, had been married before. Briefly. But it was a disaster marriage. She struggled with self-conception issues. Psychologically, she was worse off than me. My lack of self-confidence was dissipating, albeit slowly, but it was Christ working within me to strengthen me and perfect me in His image. Joni was a basket case.

This became more evident as we drew closer to our wedding day. I ignored the signs until they punched me in the face.

One night, in a bout of despair, she freaked out. Her fear of rejection caused her to sabotage the relationship. In hindsight, it wasn't a strong one to begin with. I was not the right man for her. I was not equipped to help her deal with her struggles while I still had my own. I wanted to do the right thing, but, at times, I didn't know what the right thing was.

She kept me up one night after work. I was exhausted to begin with, and it was late at night. She insisted I take my ring back.

"What? Joni, please."

She took it off her finger. "Here. Take it. You don't love me anyway."

I thought I did. Looking back, I was still fighting the sexual urges, and I could no longer ignore them. I hadn't been sexually active in a long time, but my loins were on fire. I pushed myself toward marriage with a woman I had not grown to love in the romantic sense because I had convinced myself that "it was better to marry than to burn." I didn't realize I wasn't walking by faith. I was trying to force it. I wasn't ready yet, she wasn't ready, and God hadn't prepared the right mate for either one of us.

"If I take it," I said. "You won't get it back."

"That's okay," she insisted. "Take it. I don't want it."

I looked Joni in the eye and saw nothing but fear. She was in terror. And I sensed something demonic might have been taking place, but I was powerless to deal with that. Finally, after a couple of hours of running in anxious circles around each other, I gave in.

"Okay," I said, and took the ring. I put it in my pocket and asked her to leave.

I was exasperated. She wore me out. No amount of reassuring her was going to make her believe that I accepted her just the way she was. I had to admit defeat.

After she left, I put the ring away and sat in the dark, then I prayed myself to sleep. I awoke the next morning and went to work with a broken heart.

Joni called and apologized. She wanted to get back together again. I had already thought about it. My mind was made up. I would not live with that psychosis for the rest of my life. I told her she needed to get help before she thought about getting with anyone else.

"You're not ready for marriage," I said.

"I'll be a better girlfriend," she cajoled.

"I'm sorry, Joni. You're just not ready," I said. "And I don't think I am either. I think you need professional help." And that's where I left it. Years later, she'd call and say she did just that. Got herself healthy, with professional help. And thanked me for trying to help her even though I felt like I couldn't.

i2 Technologies was a manufacturer of supply chain management software. They hired me through a temp agency to sell tickets to their conferences. I worked in a nice, plush office, a step up from what I was used to. But it was temporary work. There was talk of making some of us permanent based on performance. One of the ladies in the office and I were identified as potential candidates. We were the top performers, so they made us both floor supervisors.

My female counterpart was ambitious. She really wanted to prove herself. I wanted to continue growing in the Lord. I had given up on a writing career, but I was not satisfied being a telephone sales associate. It didn't matter that I had grown into the position, that I had learned how to quickly build a rapport with others through an impersonal mouthpiece. That was not my end destination.

I still didn't have a plan. Several years after my last foray into academia, and little time or energy for writing, I had no goal. There was nothing that I wanted, nothing I was striving for. I was simply living day to day, surviving from one moment to the next. No charted path. I didn't know where I was headed. Was this living by faith?

After a meeting where my fellow employee talked over me multiple times, she and I met with our supervisor. It was completely unrelated to the previous event, but she made a snarky comment and I let her have it. I went overboard and used some language that I shouldn't have. It shocked our boss, another female, who had been great to both of us, but she didn't like the way I spoke to my fellow employee. I didn't blame her. Later that day, I got a call from the temp agency. I was being reassigned.

That never happened. Instead, I prayed, told God I was sorry for my outburst, and asked for forgiveness. After that, I sent an email to the woman I had unloaded on and apologized for my behavior. Then I wrote a resumé.

I sent the resumé to a dozen different newspaper companies in the Dallas area in hopes of getting a job as a newspaper reporter. I hadn't done newspaper writing since high school, but at least it was a step in the right direction. I would be a writer again.

In my spirit, I had felt the call of writing for several months. But I was waiting for the National Guard to assign me a date for my officer basic course, which was required training to advance my military career. I had completed OCS, got my college degree, and had been waiting for over a year for the next leg of my training. Without it, I couldn't go any further in the Guard. I was getting impatient.

A couple of days after sending out resumes, I got a call from Today Newspapers, a small company in DeSoto, a small town just south of Dallas. They had a family of five community newspapers. Their managing editor called me in for an interview. I went thinking I might be hired as a reporter, which would have been a minimum wage hourly job. When I left the interview, I had a job as editor of one of their newspaper editions. The largest one.

Three months in, the National Guard notified me that I had a date for my required training. I spent six months at Fort Knox and went back to the newspaper. By law, they had to hold my position, or give me one of equal stature. Since they had hired another editor to take over the DeSoto paper, they offered me the Midlothian edition.

Midlothian Today was the smallest of the five community papers in the Today family, but I really liked the community. The small town was farther south, in a different county. A bedroom community made up mostly of middle-class Caucasians, a mix of white- and blue-collar professionals, and it had doubled in size in the last five years. There was a small community of Hispanics in the area, but the community was very conservative. At the time, I identified with the conservative arm of the libertarian movement, so it felt like a good placement to me.

The job was a respite to my soul. I wasn't competing with anyone for a position, I wasn't struggling to survive, and my life wasn't in turmoil. I wasn't making a lot of money, but I was happy. I had learned to be content.

One of the ways the National Guard benefitted me was providing the knowledge of what had been going on in my body for almost a decade. We were required to get a blood test or give a sample. I don't remember. It could have been a routine exam. But results came back and my platoon sergeant, Sergeant First Class Tony Williams, informed me that I had an infectious disease.

"If I, were you, sir, I'd report that to the attorney general," he advised. "That's supposed to be confidential information, but yours and Sergeant Beeman's results came back open. I wasn't supposed to see it, but I felt like you need to know."

I thanked him, but I never reported anything to the attorney general. Instead, I went to a local agency that tested and treated people with sexually transmitted diseases. They ran their own test. Sure enough, I had tertiary-stage syphilis. To treat it required three separate shots of penicillin, which I'd receive through weekly visits. One each week. I received the treatments and went on about my business.

In the tertiary stage of syphilis, there are no symptoms, but the disease is active in the body. Ultimately, it leads to brain damage if left untreated. I was lucky to have received the treatment when I did. It would eventually kill me.

While at PBC, I grew disgruntled with the emphasis on church growth. I left and began attending a Presbyterian church, PCA. I wasn't sure that's where I would land long term, but I wanted to move away from the shallow waters of "seeker sensitive" churchianity. While there, my friend Mike Bangs, a fellow poet I had met at poetry readings around Fort Worth, called and asked me if I'd help him find a church.

"Sure, I can do that," I said. After interviewing him about what kind of church he was looking for, I suggested the Episcopal church. He had rejected the Baptist and Charismatic suggestions.

"I can do Episcopal," he said. "I grew up Catholic, so I think I could fit in there."

He had been attending a nondenominational charismatic church but dropped out of that environment and was unchurched for a few months before calling me. Once we decided on the direction to go, we created a plan and executed it. We went high church.

The first church we visited was St. Alban's Episcopal Church in Arlington. It stood across the street from the University of Texas at Arlington college campus. It was practically a part of the campus.

Mike and I couldn't have been an odder fit. He stood over six feet tall and pushed three hundred pounds. He was a big, burly man with a bushy beard. He looked as if he'd recently rolled off a klondike fishing expedition. I was lean and thin. A National Guard officer, fit and short in stature, standing at just under five-eight. Clean-shaven.

As soon as we walked into the church foyer, church people dropped off the walls and descended on us like flies at a picnic. We didn't even make it into the service before an usher handed us a bulletin and a habit-sporting nun raced out of an open doorway that led to the church offices in the back. She stretched out her hand and gave us a cheery "Welcome!"

"Hi," Mike said, just as cheerily.

I felt awkward already. It seemed as if the nun had been watching us walk up to the church door on a video monitor and knew exactly when to come out to greet us. I smiled, trying to seem friendly.

"Is this your first visit with us?" the nun asked.

Mike responded. "Yes."

"Would you like to come back to our conference room? We'll tell you all about us."

That was nice. Shouldn't we experience the service, first? I thought. I followed Mike's lead.

Mike was a decade older than me, a Bible salesman by trade. He had worked for the American Bible Society for years. He was also solidly in the Arminian camp. But Mike was a good friend to me, and we would discuss theology often, sharpening each other's blade. He knew how to defend what he believed. I had more passion than sense.

We followed the nun to the conference room. She gave us some literature and Mike started asking questions.

"What's your stand on homosexuality?"

The nun didn't answer directly. She said something like, "We accept everyone as they are."

That was sufficiently vague. Mike asked it another way. She gave another cul-de-sac answer, and I tightened my sphincter wondering what the nun and her several cohorts around the table might be thinking about us at that point. We spent about thirty minutes going in circles with the lollipop auxiliary, then excused ourselves. Without attending the service, we decided that church wasn't for us. We'd try it again next week.

After a little research, I found a small Episcopal church north of town that practiced the charismatic gifts of the spirit. I thought that was an interesting mix, so we visited. The pastor was a nice guy and explained how they operate in the spirit. Mike and I both agreed that was interesting, but it wasn't for us.

Our next stop was a cathedral church in the Fort Worth diocese. We visited once and knew it was where we wanted to stay. There was no pretension, no vague belief statements, and a strong commitment to the historic tenets of the Christian faith. No compromise, no apologies, and no empty wishy-washy cultural concessions. I came to learn while we were there that the bishop in that diocese was not all that popular in the Episcopal Church of the USA. Bishop Jack Iker had a reputation for defending the orthodox faith within the Episcopal denomination, and that didn't sit well with some of the bishops in other dioceses.

It wasn't long after beginning to attend St. Vincent's Episcopal Church that I placed an ad on a dating website. I found myself scrolling through female dating profiles and found one that appealed to me. I sent a quick note to introduce myself.

I was surprised when I got a response. I had sent out introduction messages in the past and got very few responses. The responses I did get didn't make a strong case for me, usually. But this time, there seemed to be an instant rapport. After a few back-and-forth messages, Theresa and I talked on the phone a couple of times. She wanted to meet after the first call, but I put it off until after the third. We finally met face to face, and it sent me on the journey of a lifetime.

We met at a Bennigan's. Theresa ate me under the table.

"You ate everything on the plate," I said.

"Yeah!" she said. "Why waste food? You paid for it. There's no sense wasting it."

"Most women just push their food around their plate with a fork," I said. "You ate yours like it was your last meal."

She laughed. "Well, it could be."

I'd never felt as comfortable with anyone in my life as I did on that date. I put my hands on the table and looked into her eyes. She placed her hands on mine and gazed back. I felt like I was entering a whole new dimension, a universe in another person's soul.

After a couple of dates, Theresa invited me to her house for dinner. I met her three daughters, all of whom seemed excited to meet me. I brought a gift, a country music CD, and had put it in a gift bag.

"I don't know if you like country music or not," I said, "but ..."

"She does!" said Leah, about thirteen years old at the time.

"Okay, girls, don't crowd!" Theresa pushed them all out of the way and opened her gift. "They can be so annoying."

I laughed. "Actually, they're quite delightful."

I wasn't joking. I was at peace, with God and with my life. I'd even made peace with Dad. I possessed a contentedness in my spirit that surpassed everything I'd ever experienced. My life had taken many turns and had seen many ups and downs. I survived them all. I felt like I was where God wanted me to be, even if I didn't know where I was going.

That night, Theresa foisted her Pennsylvania roots on me through her cooking. When I got a taste of her homemade bread, it felt like home. She had made an impression, but it was still early on. Was this the woman I'd spend the rest of my life with? I wasn't ready for the answer, and I wasn't ready to ask that question.

I knew the answer on New Year's Eve. She was visiting with me at my house. We'd only been dating for a month, maybe a little more. While sitting on the sofa talking, I developed an earache. It was the most physically painful thing I'd ever experienced, and it was killing me.

"You want me to take you to the medical clinic?" Theresa asked.

It was a little after 10 p.m. A sharp pain shot from ear to ear, right through my brain.

"Do you mind?"

She didn't mind at all. We drove to the clinic and waited around for a couple of hours just so they could give me some antibiotics. I took them and went home. The next morning, there she was, bright and early. She had gone home to tend to her girls and came back around nine the next morning. Right about that time, my neighbor in the townhome community where I had purchased a unit, was having some plumbing work done. We shared a common wall in the living room where I was sitting, and a jackhammer from next door rattled the walls so hard I could hear it in my head. My ear ached, my brain ached, my whole body ached, and the jackhammer only made it worse.

"Come on, let's go to my house," Theresa said. And we did. I spent the entire day lying on her sofa, watching her TV, as she and her girls catered to me like I was dying from war wounds. I wasn't dying, but they made my pain bearable. At that moment, I knew I had a family.

The oldest daughter, Elizabeth, had a son who was just three months old when Theresa and I started dating. Dylan was a deal clincher for me. Suddenly, I went from being the world's most committed loner to being a part of a family in a way that I had never imagined. Well into my thirties, a committed bachelor, I was suddenly feeling familial. My own family didn't make me feel that way on most days. No church had ever made me feel that way. No one had ever made me feel like a part of a family, but Theresa and her children made me feel at home, and I think they'd have made me feel like that in the middle of the hottest desert.

We'd been dating for six months when I asked Theresa to marry me. Actually, I hinted that we should get married, but she's not good at picking up on hints.

I tried to resist, but we ended up in bed together one night. After being physical with her, I rolled over and said, "I suppose we should call the priest."

She looked at me and said, "Why? Did somebody die?"

I laughed.

"The only reason you'd call a priest is if you're burying somebody or marrying somebody," she said.

I laughed again. One of the things I've always admired about Theresa is her plain-spokenness. She doesn't clutter her language with vague suggestions and sidestepping responses, and that's refreshing in a world full of people who spend so much time not saying what they mean and going out of their way to obscure what they're thinking. Theresa has no obscurations.

"Well," I said. "I'd like to marry you."

And that was the idiot, non-romantic way I wooed my helpmate into a lifelong entanglement. It's not what I would recommend to anyone else, but it's how it happened with us. I was delighted that she accepted my proposal, and we started making plans.

She wanted to get married before Advent because, in the Episcopal church, if you don't do it before Advent, you must wait until January, after the Christmas season. The church doesn't do weddings during Advent, I learned. So, we talked to the priest, Father Cantrell, and he agreed to marry us. The following November, we adjoined our lives. Mike Bangs was my best man.

Six months after that, my Guard unit was activated, and I spent all the next year in Iraq.

I was more than inconvenienced by the war. First, it interfered with my marriage. We hadn't celebrated our first anniversary yet, and we were going to be apart for over a year. Besides that, I didn't see it as a just or necessary war. I had joined the National Guard because I wanted to be of service to my state and local communities. I had yet to be able to do that.

It was not something I handled well. After a few months of training and a year chasing the tiger's tail, I realized that I had made a big mistake in joining the Guard. It was not for me. And no one ever found weapons of mass destruction.

Every soldier joins the military knowing they may be used in ways that violates their deepest values. Members of the military train themselves to support the action even if they don't agree with the administration that enforces it. I found there were some things that I could not support. The Iraq War smacked of military imperialism to me, and it didn't make the world a better place. I believed it was ill-conceived, and when I returned home, I was bitter over it. The idyllic life I had enjoyed before the war had gone up in smoke.

I discussed my concerns with Theresa before we left stateside. She encouraged me to stick with it.

"If you don't do it, you'll regret it the rest of your life," she said.

"If I do, I may regret it just as long."

But I knew it was the right thing to perform my duty. I wanted to resign on a matter of conscience, but it didn't feel right. Throughout the deployment, I had to beat myself to do the right thing every day, and there were times when it became difficult to deal with the warmongering fervor of the soldiers in my midst. Doing one's duty was one thing, but the true believers were the ones who enjoyed it. War making is not something one should enjoy.

While I was away, Theresa moved us to Pennsylvania to be close to Dylan and the grandchild we had on the way. I joined her in December 2005, jaded and bruised.

Theresa tried her best to keep me grounded. My head hit the clouds, my heart dropped to my feet, and my spirit deflated. The plans I had made for us had been hijacked and tossed in the gutter. The life I foresaw two years earlier was a pipe dream, never to be realized. And I didn't know what to do.

God was still in control.

"I need a break," I told her. "I don't feel like doing anything right now."

I had saved ten thousand dollars while deployed, a bright spot that helped me transition back into real life. Theresa said she'd support us while I took a break. She was going to look for work online as a graphic artist while I played around on my poetry website, which I had started while in Iraq. We agreed, and then picked up life where we left off.

One month later, we had a three-year-old grandson and a one-year-old granddaughter living with us. Their mother was busy chasing Cinderella dreams. Her children needed someone who took caring for them seriously. Once again, God torqued my life like a spinning wheel.

It was difficult to get back to reality. It helped that Dylan wanted to play baseball in the backyard. Mindlessly, I went through the motions. I pitched him the ball and he'd hit it with his plastic bat. If he couldn't hit the ball, he'd get disappointed and run away to sit on the front steps of the house we were renting. I became Mr. Tenpenny to him.

I continued to play with my poetry website, creating web pages and writing a blog, but it wasn't making money. Eventually, it would earn me one hundred dollars a month for several months, which made it profitable. Barely. But that would be two years later. Until then, I had to figure out a way to earn an income. Two months after returning home from the warzone, I created a profile at Guru.com and started taking writing clients. With the savings I had and the measly income I made; I was able to sustain us for a few months. By August, we were dry.

God was the master.

I had applied to write for a website a couple of months earlier and the owner, a man named Chris McElroy, hired me to write articles for ten dollars a pop. I thought, *how am I going to make a living writing five-hundred-word articles for ten dollars each*? Since they were typically ordered in bulk, I figured out I could write ten articles on the same topic in an hour if I spent ten to fifteen minutes researching them. That translated into one hundred dollars an hour.

It was hit and miss. While the hundred dollars an hour sounds good, the monthly income was about a thousand dollars, at first. But in August, Chris called me and asked if I wanted to manage the business so he could focus on sales. I agreed.

With Theresa's help, we were able to build up the business to a decent volume within a year. We didn't get rich, but we sustained a living, and had several writers working for us most of the time. We wrote articles, blog posts, website content, and performed other services. At one time, I was making five thousand dollars a month. Not a lot, but a livable income. Then Chris disappeared.

We had worked together for several years. He discovered he was diabetic and ended up in the hospital. The first time he disappeared, for several months, I didn't know what to do. I just kept the business running. We got no new sales, but Theresa and I maintained the customer base and kept the content flowing. In two years, Chris disappeared three or four times, each time for weeks or months. Finally, I decided to go off on my own.

Meanwhile, the grandchildren were in and out of the house several times. Dylan and Savannya lived with us for a year-and-a-half before going to live with their mother. A year later, they were back with their little brother Nathen.

As chagrined as I was at having to raise someone else's children, they made life real to me. I took being the head of the family seriously. And I learned that I could be a good father, even if I wasn't a father.

Savannya would antagonize Dylan endlessly. Theresa and I would repeatedly ask her to stop doing that. Then one day, I was picking on her as she played with her dolls. She said, "Poppy, stop 'tagonizing me." Those are the moments that have motivated me to be as good a man as I can be. They are my family, and they've taught me many things. Things I could never have learned on my own.

Nathen proved to be a practical jokester. As early as one year old, he could take us unaware. Or me, at least.

One evening, he pulled at his diaper. "Do you need to change your diaper?" I asked. He couldn't speak yet, so he nodded his head. "Okay, grab a diaper and lay on the floor," I said. He did. Before I could get his diaper undone, he was laughing like a hyena. I opened the diaper. Dry and clean. After that, I've kept a very close eye on Nathen.

Having children in my home made me realize what joys I missed out on during the years of being angry at Dad. Those are years I can't get back, but God forgives. And life goes on. I look to the future, not the past.

The kids were with us for a year before they went back to their mother again. "The next time they come live with me," Theresa told Elizabeth, "I'll keep them permanently."

She said that because I wanted to keep them, I didn't want to be a yo-yo, taking the kids in and giving them back every few months. If we were going to raise someone else's children, I at least wanted the stability and permanence of knowing it was my responsibility every day. That would be good for them and better for us than the jerk around we were getting.

Raising children was how I discovered God's warped sense of humor. I had spent most of my life avoiding family. I wanted nothing to do with it. I didn't think I'd be a good father and wasn't interested in trying. Then, from out of nowhere, a tribe of kids fell out of the sky right into my pasture. And I was playing Dad whether I wanted to or not, doing my best to be a positive influence despite myself.

I'd been home from Iraq for a year when the Lord convicted me that I needed to be in church, but I knew nothing of Pennsylvania churches. The denominations were unfamiliar to me, and I didn't know what kind of church I needed to be in. I just knew I needed to be in church. I needed to be around other believers.

On a fluke, I searched for Reformed Episcopal churches. I had known someone who attended one in Texas, so I thought I'd check it out. I found a congregation in Enola, about a thirty-minute drive from our home. We attended that church for about four years before the Lord convicted me again. By that time, Dylan and Savannya were playing baseball. Theresa and I were their sponsors. The Lord told me we needed to be in a church closer to where we were active in the community.

Even when the children lived with their mother, Theresa and I stayed involved in their extracurricular activities. Their mother and her boyfriends had no interest. So, if they weren't living with us, we would drive to Elizabeth's house, pick them up, and take them wherever they needed to go. We tried very hard to give them some semblance of a normal life.

I was also a member of a writer's group in Gettysburg, and in that group was a tall wiry blond gentleman who pastored a church in Hunterstown, a small village just outside of Gettysburg.

"Let's visit Aaron's church," Theresa said. So, we did. And we stayed. In fact, we stayed for about nine years and was involved in ministry for most of that time. Theresa ran the soundboard and helped in the kitchen. I taught Sunday school, served as a lay reader and door greeter, and occasionally preached a sermon or led worship.

I've learned the Christian walk is not free of challenges. Being a Christian is the hardest thing I've ever had to do, mostly because I don't have to do anything. I've learned that God's grace is sufficient for all things, but in the daily grind, where metal beats against metal, where iron clashes with iron, there is where the sparks fly that are evidence of God's work. That is where the future kingdom of heaven breaks through into the here and now. I am not the king of that kingdom—I am not even king of my own life—but I know Him who is. And I am learning that I know Him more each day.

Discussion Questions

1) What kind of changes do you see in the author from his earlier self?

2) What do you think led to those changes?

3) Why do you think the changes were gradual and not all at once?

4) What evidence do you see of God working in his life at this stage?

REFLECTIONS

I did not write this book with malice or resentment. I wrote it with love for those who may be captured by these sentiments themselves. When I think back at decisions I've made and the motivations for making them, I realize that I allowed my own disappointments with others to dictate my choices. I wasn't free. But I found freedom in Christ.

This story is not a "tell-all" memoir. I left out many details, but I thought it important to show the kind of person I was and contrast it with who I've become, and to provide some details about my life that have influenced both. If I've done that, then I've done what I set out to do.

For years, I chased demons and dreams as if they were gods. By doing so, I ignored the true God.

I'm not good at climbing ladders, but I'm not talking about metal rungs. I mean that I've been in a variety of environments where I spent some time in leadership. That includes educational environments, the military, the nonprofit world, retail, the corporate world, and the church. In every case, even the church, I've found that the higher up in the organization one rises, the more distractions and worldly entanglements present themselves. These entanglements always looked promising until I had them, but they interfered in my relationship with God and pricked me spiritually so that I lost my focus on the things that really matter, namely, living for the Kingdom. Living for the King.

Whether it was success by worldly standards, increased wealth, prestige, physical pleasure, or pride of achievement, and whether it was in business, the craft of writing, or the promise of some other personal gain, in every case, it was an empty tomb. The only place I've ever found real, lasting enjoyment is in the presence of Jesus Christ. That's where I find joy and peace.

When I was six years old, my father took me fishing. He wanted me, for his own reasons, to learn how to fish. And I wanted to learn. When I caught a fish by the tail, he made a big deal that I had done so because I was doing it wrong. I was supposed to cast the rod into the stream and wait. At six, I didn't have the patience required to wait like a master fisherman, so I'd play with the line. He laid into me for that.

Back home, as I crawled into bed, I could hear Dad telling Mom all about it. His expectation of me was so stern it killed the desire for fishing in me. To this day, I don't care for it.

Later, when I had grandsons, they wanted to fish. Since we lived on a twenty-acre farm with a pond, I'd walk them down to the pond, bait their hooks for them, and unhook their catches for them until they were old enough to do so themselves. But I would watch them fish. I don't know whether they ever noticed that I wasn't fishing along with them. If they did, they didn't know why. Those moments were my opportunity to build equity in those relationships. I didn't need to be a master fisherman; I only needed to share the joy of that experience with my grandsons. Years later, they went to live with their mother, and I felt a void. Was I good role model? The question plagues my mind.

I've learned that one can't live through fear and doubt. Perfect love, Christ's love, casts out fear. And I know this to be true. I've experienced that love.

My desire is for other young men, and old men too—maybe even some women—who struggle with enjoying life because they have not learned to forgive someone in their past who has mistreated them will discover that they can get on with it. No one must take a vacation from living because a parent, a brother or sister, or a co-worker has made life difficult. Life will be difficult. The challenge is to live it joyously in faith despite the difficulty.

I've since learned that my parents did the best, they could in raising me. At one time, I did not understand that. It took years, but the Lord eventually revealed to me that my mission was to love and accept my father as he was. Once I could do that, I could forgive. I could overlook his faults, and my own, and enjoy his company despite our imperfections. It was a hard lesson to learn, and it took me a long time to learn it. My desire is to see other young men struggling with anger, sexual addiction, hyper ambition, and belief in God grow beyond themselves and into the man that God wants them to be.

After many years of being away, nursing the chip on my shoulder, being angry, and placing myself above the roots that pulled me toward my home, Dad and I sat together on the back porch of his East Texas home. It had once been my home. We had just finished tearing down a barbed wire fence together. A tear came to my eye as I watched him struggle to breathe.

"I love you Dad," I said, regret for past sins on my lips.

"I love you too, son."

Pushing eighty, my dad has softened. As have I. We laugh together more now than we ever have, and when he looks at me, I see a father's love. There's no time to regret not seeing it before. I see it now. And now is all that matters.

Discussion Questions

1) Did the author do a good job of showing his transformation from a young man stuck on himself to an older, more mature man with a strong faith in God?

2) When you read his story, did you get the sense that the author has asked God for forgiveness and lives that forgiveness out in his life?

3) Do you believe the author has found joy in the Lord?

4) What can you gain from Allen Taylor's testimony?

5) Do you feel empowered to share the joy of Christ with others? Are you ready to live in that power yourself?

If you find a blessing in these pages, or if you'd like to offer some feedback for my benefit, feel free to write to me at cruxpublications@gmail.com. I'd love to hear from you.

ABOUT THE AUTHOR

Allen Taylor is a published poet and fiction writer, former newspaper editor and award-winning journalist, and a professional content writer for businesses. He is a small group leader at his church, has lead worship, and has, on a few occasions, delivered a sermon. He's also smoked a few cigars. A late bloomer, he is beyond the age of fifty, married to a beautiful woman with three adult children (two of whom call him "Dad"), and is a proud Poppy to four incredible grandchildren with whom he loves to play. He is also the founder at Crux Publications, as cliché as it is (it's also true), the chief bottle washer.

ABOUT CRUX PUBLICATIONS

Crux Publications exists to serve Christian authors who want to publish books that glorify Jesus Christ. We offer three levels of service:

- ➤ Self-Publishing - For authors who want total control over their books, we'll provide the services that allow them to self-publish under their own name or fictitious entity. These services include print book and e-book formatting, book covers, editorial services, and other potential services upon request. Learn more about self-publishing with Crux Publications at https://cruxpublications.com/diy-publishing/.

- ➤ Hybrid Publishing - Our hybrid publishing model is a partnership between publisher and author. While the author has more control over the finished product than with traditional publishing, as publisher, we provide our knowledge of the publishing industry to create book covers, format print books and e-books, and perform other publishing services without expense to the author in exchange for a piece of the royalty pie. Hybrid publishers are known to offer authors higher royalties than traditional publishers. Crux Publications' royalty schedule is generous even for hybrid publishers. Learn more about hybrid publishing with Crux Publications at https://cruxpublications.com/hybrid-publishing/.

- ➤ Testimonies - The Crux Publications Testimonies imprint allows authors to tell their faith story and submit a manuscript for review. If we accept your testimony, we'll publish it at our expense and pay you higher royalties than traditional publishing contracts. Learn more about publishing your Christian testimony with Crux Publications at https://cruxpublications.com/publish-your-testimony/.

Receive regular commentary on living the Christian life, written by Crux Publications founder and published Allen Taylor. Follow the The Crux newsletter (it's free) at thecrux.substack.com.

Current Crux Publications titles include:

- ➤ The Voice of the Broken by Melissa Hurd

- ➤ I Am Not The King (A Personal Testimony of My Growth in Jesus Christ) by Allen Taylor

More titles are on the way. You can find Crux Publications at https://cruxpublications.com/books-by-crux-publications/.

Made in the USA
Middletown, DE
18 September 2024

60622422R00046